The University of Chicago

THE CAMPUS GUIDE

The University of Chicago

AN ARCHITECTURAL TOUR BY

Jay Pridmore

WITH PHOTOGRAPHS BY
Peter Kiar

FOREWORD BY
Don Michael Randel

Princeton Architectural Press

NEW YORK | 2006

Princeton Architectural Press
37 East Seventh Street
New York, New York 10003

For a free catalog of books, call 1.800.722.6657.
Visit our web site at www.papress.com.

The essay "The University of Chicago and the American College Campus" by Neil Harris first appeared in Jean Block, *The Uses of Gothic: Planning and Building the Campus of the University of Chicago 1892–1932* (University of Chicago Press, 1983).

Photo credits:
All images by Peter Kiar unless otherwise noted.
Pages xii, 1, 3–6, 8, 44: Special Collections Research Center, University of Chicago Library
Page 57 bottom: Marc PoKempner
Page 74: Alex S. MacLean
Page 103 bottom: Dennis Fiser
Pages 112, 116–117, 119–120: Alex G. MacLean
Pages 123, 135: Dennis Fiser
Page 144: Gregory Gaymont

Series editor: Nancy Eklund Later
Series concept: Dennis Looney
Project editor and layout: Nicola Bednarek
Maps: Jane Sheinman

Special thanks to: Nettie Aljian, Dorothy Ball, Janet Behning, Penny (Yuen Pik) Chu, Russell Fernandez, Jan Haux, Clare Jacobson, John King, Mark Lamster, Linda Lee, Katharine Myers, Lauren Nelson, Scott Tennent, Jennifer Thompson, Paul G. Wagner, Joseph Weston, and Deb Wood of Princeton Architectural Press —Kevin C. Lippert, publisher

Library of Congress Cataloging-in-Publication Data
Pridmore, Jay.
   The University of Chicago : an architectural tour / by Jay Pridmore;
with photographs by Peter Kiar.
      p. cm. — (The campus guide)
   Includes bibliographical references and index.
   ISBN 1-56898-447-2 (alk. paper)
      1. University of Chicago—Guidebooks. 2. University of Chicago—Buildings.
   I. Title. II. Series: Campus guide (New York, N.Y.)
LD931.P75 2006
378.773'11—dc22
                                                                    2005021316

Printed and bound in China

How to Use This Book

This guide is for anyone who wishes to visit and understand the architecture at the University of Chicago and its rich history.

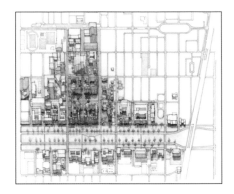

As a means of organization, the book divides the campus and portions of its neighborhood into nine walking tours. Some walks are self-contained, such as Walks Five ("South of the Midway") and Six ("Medical Center"). Others are more arbitrarily selected, such as the division of the Main Quadrangles into three different walks through seven interconnecting courtyards. In all cases, the walks constitute a useful itinerary to the physical campus and its architectural history.

Visitors are welcome to tour the University of Chicago campus:
The office of college admissions provides regular tours of the campus, at 10:30 a.m. from December to February, and at 10:30 a.m. and 1:30 p.m. from March to November. Saturday tours are given from late September through late November at 9 and 11 a.m. For more details, call 773-702-8650 or visit the university's website: www.uchicago.edu.

The Smart Museum, with the university's extensive art collection, at 5550 Greenwood Avenue, is open Tuesday through Friday 10 a.m. to 4 p.m. (open until 8 p.m. Call 773-702-0200 for information. Thursdays during the school year); Saturday and Sunday 11 a.m. to 5 p.m. Admission is free.

The Renaissance Society, a gallery of contemporary art, in 418 Cobb Hall, is open Tuesday through Friday 10 a.m. to 5 p.m.; Saturday and Sunday noon to 5 p.m. Call 773-702-8670 for information. Admission is free.

The Oriental Institute Museum, with artifacts and exhibitions of the ancient Near East, at 1155 East 58th Street, is open Tuesday through Saturday 10 a.m. to 6 p.m. (open until 8:30 p.m. Wednesday); Sunday noon to 6 p.m. Call 773-702-9514 for information or visit www.oi.uchicago.edu. Admission is free.

Tours of Robie House, 5757 South Woodlawn Avenue, are given by the Frank Lloyd Wright Preservation Trust weekdays at 11 a.m., 1 p.m. and 3 p.m., weekends every 20 minutes from 11 a.m. to 3:30 p.m. Tours of the house are $12 for adults, $10 for students and seniors. Tours of the immediate neighborhood are also given. Call 773-834-1847 for information.

Acknowledgments

This book is the most recent effort to chronicle the history of the university's architecture, which has been a continuing source of pride for many connected to the University of Chicago. The project was initiated by Larry Arbeiter, director of University Communications, and it received vital support from the staff of the University Publications office, beginning with its director, Julie Robinson, and its art director, Cynthia Bold. They were indispensable in bringing this book to publication.

Photographs by Peter Kiar represent the work of several years and they, happily, speak for themselves.

Also key to the production of this book was our editor at Princeton Architectural Press, Nicola Bednarek, whose clear eye and limitless patience were invaluable at every step and very much appreciated.

Many people contributed to its early planning and research. A committee was established to oversee the book's production, and it included Professors Neil Harris and Michael Conzen, Trustee Robert Feitler, and former university architect Curt Heuring. Professor Harris's reading of the manuscript was invaluable, as was that of Bill Murphy, a historian who had previously served as assistant vice president of news and publications at the university.

Others connected to the university were also generous in assisting the author in researching and writing this guide. Among them were staff members of the Department of Special Collections at the Regenstein Library, including Director Alice Schreyer, University Archivist Dan Meyer, and Julia Gardner. The author also interviewed Professor Geoffrey Stone, who was Provost when most of the newest buildings on campus were planned; Facilities Planners Mary Anton, Richard Bumstead, Dahlia Boyd, and Jim Hietbrink; and Campus Architects Ken Park and Rakesh Kumar. A number of people with special knowledge about areas of buildings were also helpful, including John Easton of the university hospitals, Houston Patterson of the special events office, and Jim Waters, an undergraduate math major whose enthusiasm and knowledge about stone-carved ornament around the university were extremely valuable.

Several architects and designers were helpful in the research of this book. They included Harry Ellenzweig and Neil Cahalane at Ellenzweig Associates, master stone carver Walter Arnold, and Betsy Beaman at Stanley Beaman and Sears.

Jay Pridmore

Foreword

At the University of Chicago, ideas matter. And we should not neglect the fact that architecture forms part of the world of ideas. It is, or ought to be, one of humankind's noblest activities, since it is one of the traces that we leave for those who come after us of what we thought and valued. In this way, architecture is not mere ornament but it is profoundly revealing. At a university, architecture must above all else aspire to ideas that are worthy to be part of the debate that the institution stands for. (In this context I must recall what I tell my students on writing about music: "I like it" and "I don't like it" do not count as ideas and thus do not usefully contribute to debate worthy of the name.) The quality of our architecture should be equal to that of our physics, medicine, economics, or philosophy departments. We should want to build buildings that are worth arguing about rather than buildings that few will ever notice.

This need not entail a squandering of resources, as has sometimes been claimed. Great architecture can be achieved within sensible financial constraints, though this requires both a great architect and a great client. Unfortunately, universities can be difficult clients; with their diffuse authority, they may have difficulty articulating clearly their requirements or making the many choices among competing ideas that any project is sure to entail. But universities today are the institutions most likely to be the patrons of great architecture, and they should not shrink from the responsibility this imposes. It is a responsibility to the history of civilization, and it is a responsibility to their own history as custodians of the record of human accomplishment.

At the University of Chicago, we create architecture primarily in order to enhance our ability to develop the kinds of ideas that matter. In that sense, a building is only as good as the ideas that are generated in it. For example, one of our newest buildings houses our Graduate School of Business, a place where ideas matter and which has generated ideas that matter. Finance is now conducted worldwide in fundamentally new ways that rest on ideas developed in the Graduate School of Business, and we celebrate this great new building because it will house the continuing, spirited debate that produces ideas that change the world.

Thanks to our thoughtful predecessors, the architectural record of this campus is overall a respectable part of our intellectual tradition. The Gothic-inspired buildings of our earliest days are genuine originals and not the slavish imitations that came into vogue somewhat later. And every generation since is represented by work of talented and distinguished practitioners. If there is change in the university's architecture over time, it is in the way in which our buildings, like the university itself, address the surrounding community. The Gothic impulse created a community turned inward and away from an outside world that, in the Middle Ages and indeed in some parts of the twentieth century, was seen as dangerous. Our most recent buildings project a much greater openness and a welcoming spirit to the surrounding community. Alumni House, a historic building recently acquired, welcomes alumni and visitors from around the world and, through its location, blurs the physical boundary of the campus. Even further extensions of the physical reach of our campus include the Gleacher Center in the heart of downtown Chicago as well as facilities in Singapore and London.

Let us hope that our successors one hundred years from now will be able to take as much pride in what we leave behind as we now take in the work of our predecessors. In the meantime, we welcome to the campus all who care about architecture—to study it, admire it, one hopes, but in any case to debate it.

Don Michael Randel
President, University of Chicago

TOP: *University of Chicago campus, looking southeast from west of Ellis Avenue, 1905*
BOTTOM: *Main Quadrangles, ca. 1916*

LEFT: *John D. Rockefeller*
RIGHT: *William Rainey Harper*

Introduction

In little more than a century, the University of Chicago has grown from its beginnings as a grand idea into an institution that has, if anything, exceeded its ambitions. The earliest plans of its founders were hardly modest, as they charted a research university of international stature. Though established by Baptists, its programs would not be limited, nor even much influenced, by religious doctrine. Instead, its objective was to influence society at large through the systematic discovery of new knowledge.

The university's success was almost immediate: With the resources of John D. Rockefeller, the principal founder, and the vision of William Rainey Harper, the first president, it attracted leading scholars from all over the country; professors with secure positions elsewhere—and this included Harper himself—joined the faculty entirely on the strength of the university's promise. Donors contributed more than $2 million by the time Chicago opened, and the student body on opening day amounted to more than seven hundred undergraduates and graduates from all over the world. Keys to the success of such an enterprise are many, but the strength of the university's original program was certainly a major factor. Hardly ever had such an institution been created with so elaborate and precise a blueprint for what "higher learning," as Harper called it, could achieve. And rarely did one stay so thoroughly on course. Elements included plans for a wide range of academic departments, a commitment to research, the establishment of affiliations, and, of course, a stately physical plant.

Gothic origins

Besides establishing guidelines for the university's academic goals, one of the founders' first decisions involved the new institution's look. They strongly felt that the campus architecture should express both the university's unity of approach and its interdisciplinarity of thinking. They soon resolved to create a complete system of quadrangles that would in time be lined with gray stone buildings designed in the Gothic manner. As many as forty Gothic revival buildings on the original quadrangles would bind together "into a unity the many complex and diverging forms of activity which constitute university life," serving many functions and disciplines but visibly being part of one whole.

The Gothic style was also well suited to reflect the timelessness of the university's educational mission. The desire to emphasize the institution's apparent "age" was so strong that Harper actually proposed to forego inaugural ceremonies. He hoped, instead, that the university's first day, October 1, 1892, should appear "a continuation of a work that had been conducted for a thousand years." In fact, a short service was held in Cobb Hall, but more important than any speeches on that occasion was the solid and ancient profile of the one building ready for occupancy.

The designs of the early buildings were indeed so satisfactory that the Gothic revival style was repeated almost without lapse for nearly fifty years. The fidelity to the original plan over more than four decades, with at least four different major architects engaged, would amaze architects in later years. "Imagine what would have happened," wrote Eero Saarinen, consulting university architect in the 1950s, "if three or four equally eminent architects of our day were asked to do four sides of a square."

Naturally enough, not everyone endorsed the Gothic. Some found the antique ambiance of this campus out of step with a place that strove for advanced research. Economist Thorstein Veblen, whose most famous work is the *Theory of the Leisure Class* and who taught at the university from 1892 to 1906, cited "the disjointed grotesqueries of an eclectic and modified Gothic," which would end up regrettable when the style fell from fashion. On the contrary, the Gothic campus has aged well and its architecture has long stood as an emblem of the university's deeper purpose.

Foundations

The original resolution for the University of Chicago came not from native Chicagoans but from the American Baptist Education Society, a council of (mostly Eastern) Baptist leaders. While the society's primary concern was the training of new ministers, at a meeting in Washington, D.C. in 1888, they resolved that "the establishment of a thoroughly equipped Baptist

Rockefeller and Harper at the decennial of the University of Chicago, 1901

institution of learning in Chicago is an immediate and imperative denominational necessity."

The Baptists were certainly motivated by the fact that Chicago
proper lacked a major institution of higher education at the time. A previous Baptist institution, the "old" University of Chicago, was founded in 1857
on land donated by Senator Stephen Douglas, but it never attained solvency
and despite programs in law, medicine, and other areas, was closed in 1886.
Instead of being discouraged by that failure, the Baptists seized an opportunity to do what the Methodists and Presbyterians had done in Evanston and
Lake Forest—to found an institution of large scale and broad scope.

It was no mere coincidence that their uncommonly successful new
university would grow in Chicago, a city of uncommon ambition and energy.
In this place, builders really did "make no little plans," as Daniel Burnham
later exhorted in his 1909 *Plan of Chicago*. It is true that the elaborate Gothic
architecture of the campus appears little related to the buildings that made
Chicago a great architectural center at the time—home of the skyscraper,
the "commercial style," and the Prairie School, made famous by Frank Lloyd
Wright. On reflection, however, it is clear that the builders of the university
were driven by ambitions as intense and ineluctable as those of the builders
of the city at large.

Other conditions also encouraged the Baptists to think in large
terms. Principal among them was the potential beneficence of oil magnate
John D. Rockefeller, who was an active Baptist and by the 1880s appeared

Perspective drawing of Henry Ives Cobb's master plan for the university, 1893

ready to distribute his massive fortune. Denominational leaders approached Rockefeller for support of their new educational enterprise, and he eventually agreed to an initial contribution of $600,000, which would later widen to tens of millions of dollars.

Also essential in the dramatis personae was William Rainey Harper, a professor of ancient languages and a Baptist minister teaching at Yale at this time. From the beginning, plans for a new institution of higher learning involved the young scholar. Rockefeller and Harper were of essentially the same mind when it came to plans for their new university, though both were tough with one another. Rockefeller was initially insisting that his contributions be matched by others. Harper, on the other hand, was relentless in going to Rockefeller for more money whenever required. On one famous visit, Rockefeller received Harper on the sole condition that there would be no request for a check on this occasion. Harper instead turned their meeting into a prayer that was so long and so filled with the university's urgent need that Rockefeller relented and handed over however many hundreds of thousands the university needed that day.

An Enduring Plan

The founding of the university also involved many non-Baptists, and it is to several of these—native Chicagoans who believed in the need for such an institution—that primary credit goes for the architectural character of the university. They included Martin Ryerson and Charles Hutchinson, both heirs to great fortunes who became central figures in several of the city's cultural organizations. As original members of the Committee for Buildings and Grounds, Ryerson and Hutchinson held their first meeting (along with Thomas Wakefield Goodspeed, Secretary of the Board of Trustees) nine

LEFT: *Henry Ives Cobb*
RIGHT: *Martin Ryerson*

days after the university received its charter in 1890. Without delay, they set about to determine where to build the first buildings and what those buildings would look like.

The committee undertook this charge with remarkable vision, first trading parts of donated land and buying other parcels to assemble a four-square-block central campus facing the Midway. It would be years before this area was filled with buildings, but the trustees professed patience. Hutchinson, in particular, thought that the failure of some Chicago institutions was in their unwillingness to think big, and that this was what most likely doomed the first "University of Chicago."

To devise a true master plan for the new campus, the committee engaged architect Henry Ives Cobb, chosen from among several local firms. Cobb was more eclectic, and perhaps derivative, than Chicago's trailblazing figures such as John Root or Louis Sullivan (who did not apply for the commission). Yet, for the university, he did brilliantly, quickly devising a scheme of seven quadrangles, six of generally equal size around a larger central court. The quadrangles were tailored to suit the variety of functions required— dormitories in some, laboratories and classrooms in others. While simple and seemingly obvious today, this plan could be completed gradually by deliberate accretion, a principle that was central to the design of the functioning university. It also created in substantial isolation a place where thoughtful study could be conducted undisturbed by "the dark congestions of the mercantile city," as H. G. Wells wrote in an article after a visit to Chicago in 1906.

For the design of the buildings, Cobb had the background to provide any of a number of styles. Prior to this commission, his best-known works included a Romanesque building for the Newberry Library and a

LEFT: *The early campus as seen from the world fair's Ferris Wheel, 1893*
RIGHT: *Departmental library in Cobb Hall, mid-1890s*

flamboyant Venetian Gothic structure for the Chicago Athletic Association. The architect's first rendering for the university (an unspecified structure that was not built) involved a sprawling but symmetrical mass with rusticated walls and massive arches. The design was Richardsonian Romanesque, a then popular style identified with Boston architect Henry Hobson Richardson, who died in 1886. But this proposal was rejected by the trustees who, of course, had other ideas for the campus. "The very latest English Gothic" was how Hutchinson put his preference.

Resembling the European models of Oxford and Cambridge, the Gothic revival was a plausible choice for the courtyards and cloisters that the trustees imagined. But beyond mere imitation of these five-hundred-year-old institutions, the Gothic scheme adopted by the university was a logical result of the intellectual climate at the time. Widely read writers such as William Morris and John Ruskin were at once sharp critics of industrialized society and vociferous admirers of good design, and in this spirit they promoted a new appreciation for medieval craftsmanship in everything from bookbinding to buildings.

It was also no mere coincidence that the university's planning coincided with another architectural event of power and authority, the World's Columbian Exposition. The world's fair had been approved by Congress in 1890 and had been allocated land in Jackson Park and the Midway Plaisance, adjacent to the new university's site. The exposition was enormously influential to the university. For one thing, the close proximity gave the institution a prominence, and perhaps a prestige, that it might not otherwise have enjoyed. Perhaps equally important, the Columbian Exposition became a stylistic counterpoint to the university's architecture. In direct contrast, perhaps even in competition with the fair's shimmering neoclassicism, the trustees planned an elaborate campus in the quieter but no-less-stately Gothic. Hyde Park thus became the stage for an architectural "battle of styles" that was then going on in America. On one side was the neoclassical as taught by the Ecole des Beaux-Arts in Paris; its imperial overtones and palatial scale made it the preferred style of industrial barons. On the other was the Gothic revival, an approach that was less rigid, more personal, stressed craftsmanship, and projected a more spiritual tone.

The Gothic style at large, and the late-Gothic English Perpendicular, in particular, turned out to be a propitious choice. We shall see that it embraced many "organic" principles that were commonly invoked in architecture at the time, particularly by Sullivan and Wright in their own modern ways. For example, Gothic form could be made suitable for almost any function—a weather tower in Rosenwald Hall, a system of bridges to connect Harper Library to reading rooms in other buildings, and even a medical center that maximized fresh air and sunlight, considered indispensable in modern hospital design.

Gothic architecture also provided a signature for the university that proved durable, even after the overbearing onset of twentieth-century modernism. After Cobb's tenure ended in 1901, the Boston firm of Sheply, Rutan and Coolidge continued the Gothic tradition; with increased funding from Rockefeller for the prospering university, their elaborate designs were modeled more closely than ever on "Oxbridge." Other architects such as Holabird and Roche also designed successful Gothic revival buildings, even as modern influences seeped into their designs.

The "Modern" Era

By the 1940s, the Gothic revival was no longer in fashion, for better or worse, but the gables and gargoyles of the quadrangles remained the university's immutable symbol. The old template had a particularly profound effect on Eero Saarinen, who became consulting architect to the university in 1954, commissioned by President Lawrence Kimpton primarily to create a master plan for its expansion. Saarinen arrived as an unabashed modernist but assumed an emphatic affection for the existing campus, which was of course anything but modern. While the construction of more "revival" buildings was out of the question under Saarinen, his planning work for the university recognized the Gothic past in many salubrious ways. He called for more open spaces and courtyards to augment the originals. Perhaps most boldly, he imagined the Midway Plaisance as a vast quadrangle, enclosed on the north with existing buildings and on the south with mostly new ones.

Saarinen's plan was immensely ambitious and perhaps even quixotic. It would be difficult enough to reroute traffic that normally used the Midway as an artery—Saarinen's scheme for such a change went unrealized. But the biggest challenge of the Saarinen years was to cultivate (in his own work and that of other architects who received commissions) a style that would blend modernity with the existing spirit of the campus. In fact, a design of Saarinen's own, among a long line of modern buildings on the south edge of the Midway, is a rare success in this respect. His D'Angelo Law Library, part of the Laird Bell Law Quadrangle (1959), embodies modernist ideals,

Fifty-fifth Street renovation, 1960

appearing ethereal and seemingly weightless, yet coexists in substantial harmony with the older Gothic Burton-Judson dormitories next door.

Unfortunately, there were no reprisals of the D'Angelo Law Library. Saarinen's premature death in 1961 coincided with the perceived need by the university to reassess, or at least adjust, its building program. Modern architecture of this era had failed to make a positive impact on a campus where architecture had always generated pride. (Even Saarinen's now-demolished Woodward Court Dormitories, completed in 1958, were unloved for their cinder-block economies.) But more important than matters of style, was the administration's attention to the immediate Hyde Park neighborhood. The area around campus, once one of the university's strengths, was now falling into severe decline. So serious was the perception of poverty and crime on the edges of campus that there were some proposals, however fleeting, to move the university altogether—to California, some suggested, or to the most unlikely destination of Aspen. Leaving Chicago was out of the question, naturally, so the next most radical solution was "urban renewal," engineered largely by the university under President Kimpton and a citizens organization called the South East Chicago Commission.

A recitation of Hyde Park's urban renewal story demonstrates how times, tastes, and ideas about political correctness have shifted since that ambitious project. At that time, university publications promoting urban renewal frequently juxtaposed pictures of old, ramshackle buildings with renderings or actual photos of the sleek modern designs that were replacing them. Without even considering the politics of gentrification, what is striking about these illustrations is how handsome some "slum" buildings might have become if restored, and how dated and unappealing their concrete surrogates are today.

Related to the urban renewal of the 1960s was another milestone of campus design: a partial shift in its orientation. With Fifty-fifth Street now cleared, planners produced schemes for new buildings and courtyards that opened, at least slightly, to the outside world to the north. Among these plans, a "student village" scheme by Edward Larrabee Barnes included new courtyards, different from the old in that they were not hermetically sealed and had broad openings onto Fifty-fifth Street. These ideas were only partly executed, with the Cochrane-Woods Art Center (1974) and the Court Theater (1981) going up not far from the first new dormitory to be built in twenty-seven years, Pierce Tower (1960).

Another major push in this era was for new science facilities, part of a national obsession after America's shock at the Soviets' launch of Sputnik, the first satellite in space. Federal money was made available as rarely before in Washington's effort to win the cold war by educating more and better scientists. But while the cost of more building was not a problem in this period, retaining a high architectural standard was never an easy matter. The first two laboratories built on what would become the Science Quadrangle were Hinds (1968) and Cummings (1973). Both by I. W. Colburn, they will not be mistaken for masterpieces, though they exhibit an effort to reference the past while addressing current needs. In fact, these are conspicuous (perhaps overly so) milestones of the architectural style that was fashionable when they were built: "Brutalism," which was named after Le Corbusier's highly regarded designs in *béton brut*, or raw concrete.

One cannot discuss this period without making mention of the Regenstein Library (1970), whose modern and mildly brutalist design appeared out of place when it was first built amidst the carved Gothic stone of the campus around it. But to the credit of the library's architect, Walter Netsch of Skidmore, Owings and Merrill, it has proven highly functional, and its open courtyard, on axis with Cobb Gate, serves as a well-traveled artery of pedestrian traffic. As the Regenstein's architectural eccentricities have become increasingly familiar and less jarring, it becomes more and more apparent that its seemingly random layout has a picturesque logic, and that the building is curiously in keeping with the Gothic character of the old campus across the street.

Today, campus expansion continues apace under President Don Randel, who succeeded his predecessor Hugo Sonnenschein in 2000. Campus buildings of the twenty-first century are going up at a pace not experienced in decades. And in many ways the spectral presence of history is as imposing now as it was when the university was new. As much as ever, the architects of the present aspire to recognize and enhance, although not imitate, the Gothic elements that inspired the original.

The Promise of the Future

Recent architects—even, and perhaps especially, "starchitects"—commissioned for major buildings of late have been keenly aware that new architecture is successful as it echoes the essence of the old campus while serving new needs with innovative buildings. They understand that the university's character is still, and should remain, a place of intimate courtyards, predominantly perpendicular building designs, and conspicuous craftsmanship in the construction. Their question, of course, is how to address this in contemporary terms.

There have been miscalculations. The new Press Building (Laurence Booth, 2001) south of the Midway shows that postmodern references such as pointed arches in faux-limestone are simply unsatisfying in contemporary design. Architecture can and must do more. Happily, other examples of recent modern architecture can be judged successful, blending advanced building technique and meaningful artistic expression. Cesar Pelli, whose brilliant career owes as much to sheer practicality as aesthetic daring, designed the new Ratner gym (2003) with pylons that soar like gothic towers. By the same token, Riccardo Legorreta chose brick for his Palevsky Commons dormitories (2003), which was an unexpected choice (as was his palette of bright pastels) in an age of precast concrete, but an interesting one that sets the dorms more in the context of the neighborhood around the campus than that of the quadrangles at its core. Perhaps most provocatively, the glass and steel of Rafael Viñoly's Graduate School of Business (2004) attempts to echo the horizontal lines of Robie House and the soaring Gothic arches of Rockefeller Memorial Chapel, both nearby.

Still other works of new campus architecture succeed less because of striking or innovative form and more because of utter suitability to function. Among these is the Center for Integrative Science (Ellenzweig Associates, 2008), which deftly serves the university's age-old emphasis on crossing disciplinary boundaries. The CIS, as it is called, appears workmanlike if unexciting on its exterior, but this sprawling laboratory building was designed carefully from the inside out to promote interaction among scientists in different fields.

Now buildings of the future are on the drawing board, which, by appearance, keep the past in mind but also address the deeply felt needs of the future. Among major projects are changes south of the Midway where new undergraduate residences and an expanded School of Social Service Administration complex are either under construction or in serious planning phases. Schemes for these projects indicate that the university, once an ivory tower, now seeks a more active relationship with its neighbors. Especially in areas where fear and physical barriers previously characterized town-gown relations, architects are grappling with an invigorating question: how to maintain the courtyard atmosphere that has served the university so well for so long, yet also open the campus to neighboring communities.

Whatever other elements of history this book illuminates, it should stress the importance of architecture to the intellectual well-being of the University of Chicago at large. Early campus architecture was central to the ideas of Harper, Rockefeller, and the founding trustees who sought a single spirit in a university of many parts. Its middle years revealed an institution struggling with new economic realities, untried construction technologies, and experimental architectural styles. Of recent architecture, the best new designs on campus represent truly thoughtful attempts to tie the rich past of the university's campus to its dynamic future. It will simply take time to know whether these dramatic buildings measure up to that high but achievable standard.

The University of Chicago and the American College Campus by **Neil Harris**

According to most dictionaries "college campus" is an Americanism whose roots go back to the eighteenth century. Although word origins are not always trustworthy guides to cultural history there is a certain appropriateness to this one. For the college campus has long occupied a special status within the American landscape.

One reason is purely negative. It faced little competition. The youth, poverty, scale, and voluntarism of most American institutions argued against the construction of impressive ensembles, at least through the late nineteenth century. Few military, clerical, or fraternal foundations could dot the scene with the lavish structures and cultivated acreage they enjoyed in Europe. Castles, cathedrals, and fortresses were rarely met in the United States, and picturesque ruins were accessible only to tourists who journeyed back across the Atlantic, or south to Mexico and Central America.

The college campus took on special meaning for a second reason: the power of numbers. By the early nineteenth century the United States contained more colleges than several European countries combined. Religious convictions, state rivalries, and fears of cultural degeneration stimulated an unprecedented flurry of college creations. More than four hundred institutions were functioning when the University of Chicago was founded.

Of course claiming the title of college or university, like calling any motley collection of buildings and grounds a campus, could be an ambitious arrogation. Like city plans American campus schemes even when born in grandiose hopes, usually collapsed into compromise and confusion. The conception Jefferson developed for the University of Virginia came early on the national scene, and it was never surpassed, setting a standard for later experiments. But the brilliant Charlottesville idea produced few imitators. However numerous their company or sentimental the loyalties they stimulated, most American colleges grew by accretion. They rarely possessed either the money or the patience to work things out from the start.

Neither palatial nor quadrangular, departing from both the English and the Continental ideals, the American college featured rambling and often ill-defined grounds. Not without charm, particularly in small towns and country villages, campuses were peppered by lecture halls, Old Mains, pinnacled libraries, chapels, dormitories, and observatories. Writing with only measured sympathy about the old Harvard Yard in 1909, the architectural critic Montgomery Schuyler argued that the successive buildings were placed "wherever they could go without any thought whatsoever of their relation to one another. Neither in the ground plan nor in the actual aspect is there anything to be made out but higgledy-piggledy. There is no grouping, there are no vistas." Exceptions like Virginia, Union College in Schenectady, and Hartford's Trinity only emphasized the point more clearly.

Until the 1880s this was where things stood. But the changes which came in the following decade were broad as they were sudden. Comprehensive schemes for Columbia, Berkeley, N.Y.U., Washington University, West Point, Stanford, and Chicago altered the university presence permanently. In 1888 James Bryce noted, almost parenthetically, that the new college buildings he had seen on his American trip were handsome and useful. He said little else about them. But by 1903, as *The Nation* pointed out in an editorial entitled "The College Beautiful," Bryce would have had to take more extended notice of the audacious plans under way. New institutions had the greatest scope, of course, but older colleges like Harvard, Yale, Penn, Amherst, Princeton, and Williams were also engaged in building extensive additions for themselves from the menu of Collegiate Gothic, Neo-Classic, and Renaissance forms offered them by their architects.

The American fin-de-siècle favored large plans. Encouragement for campus planning grew, as new landscapes multiplied. Besides Chicago's Columbian Exposition, a close neighbor to the university, there were huge fairs in Omaha, Buffalo, and St. Louis. These fairs coincided with—and helped stimulate—massive new planning schemes for Cleveland, Chicago, San Francisco, Washington, D.C., Denver, and Minneapolis, most of them worked on after the century's end. There were the enormous new railroad stations like Grand Central and Pennsylvania in New York, Chicago's Northwestern, and Washington's Union Station, along with impressive museums, libraries, hospitals, and office structures, all adding dramatic monumentality (and cloistered enclaves) to the national scene.

Some of this building activity between 1890 and 1910 bespoke the mere pressure of numbers and the stress of expansion. Rising population, changing technologies, and expanded transport required systematic ordering for minimal levels of efficiency and comfort. But the concert for landscaped harmony demonstrated something else, less specific but equally insistent, the intrusion of an aesthetic mandate. The haphazard, incongruous, and ill-fitting aspects of both city and countryside mocked the wealth and pretensions of many communities and appeared to threaten their stated ideals. In financial resources, size, and potential influence American institutions could compete with counterparts in Britain and Germany. Paintings, books, professors, even scholarly values were importable, to supplement what was already available. But until physical expression suited good taste and testified to permanence and cultural commitment, the institutions would be limited in their power. "Respect for the natural beauty and architectural possibility of its site is the measure of the culture of an institution," *The Nation* insisted. Seemly buildings displayed intellectuality "as plainly as dress betrays the wearer."

Many American colleges felt a lack of fit between purpose and posture in the 1890s. One source for the failure of American higher education to exert greater influence on contemporary life could be lain to the physical environment. Self-respect demanded scale and harmony. Architectural planning was no superfluity or costly luxury indulged only after other needs had been met. Expenditure and intelligent design were ways to cement loyalty and encouraged those high principles that might counter the materialism that threatened community life. Progressive reformers, along a broad spectrum of interests, acknowledged with new enthusiasm the instrumental possibilities of the landscape.

The creation of Chicago's campus in the 1890s, then, was not anomalous. It fit squarely the new national concern for environmental effect. Special aspects of the Chicago scheme did add their own emphases. Jean Block outlines several in her book *The Uses of Gothic* the continuity of the interested trustees, their need to assure potential supporters that this second University of Chicago would stay the course, the clarity of their English collegiate architecture which served as their model. But two features of the Chicago plan transcend particularity.

One concerned its immediate surroundings. The village of Hyde Park had been annexed by the city of Chicago just a couple of years before the university began. American universities would, increasingly, have close ties with, if not actual location in, large cities. Bt while it was in the city, the University of Chicago was not firmly of the city. Suburban in character, flat, unornamented, still largely treeless, its local landscape offered few scenic highlights. The one exception was the great lakefront, a short walk away. Jefferson's University of Virginia lay open at one end to the agreeable Virginia countryside, inviting its students and faculty to gaze out on a scene that, to Jefferson at least, summoned up the symbols of republican yeomanry. But this does not exist in Chicago. No Cam, no Isis, no Rhine, no Seine, no mountaintops or sacred groves beckoned to young scholars. The university intended to provide its own landscape; or at least it gave evidence that it would do so eventually.

The campus, therefore, began from its perimeters rather than its center, creating its boundaries and marking off its territory. In the first years this meant incongruities and strange separations. As Dean George E. Vincent explained in a 1902 magazine article, because of the presence of "a final plan, a few buildings may seem isolated, and here and there unfinished." The distances were sometimes more magnificent than the structures. But it meant also a certain degree of spaciousness, whatever the sacrifice of historic growth. As early as 1906 H. G. Wells could comment on the trees and green spaces, "a wonderful contrast to the dark congestions of the mercantile city of the north. To all the disorganization of that it is even physically antagonistic." Like many future institutions the university confronted its relationship to the outer world by emphasizing discontinuity rather than unhindered access. Despite the many ties that would develop to both the downtown and the urban netherworld, the campus would remain a place apart. There were dangers here, of course. But also advantages. Viewing the walls and gates of another American campus in 1904, Henry James noted the way in which "the formal enclosure of objects at all interesting immediately refines upon their interest." It "establishes values." Creating such precincts resembled, in the social order, "the improved situation of the foundling who has discovered his family or of the actor who has mastered his part." In view of the growing importance of alumni ties and academic ceremonial, James's incorporation of domestic and theatrical imagery was prescient. The campus was a stage and it needed its boundaries.

The other feature of Chicago's plan was its uniformity. Gothic permitted variation and idiosyncrasy but it set the general tone. In later years critics ranging from Thorstein Veblen to Upton Sinclair would pillory the strange spectacle of modern scientific research taking place within a medieval dream facade. The conjunction of gargoyles and test tubes seemed hard to accept. Yet the architectural homogeneity was in part a response to the new institution's bewildering diversity. Specialization of function, abstruseness of expertise, mutual incomprehension of scholarly inquirers bothered patrons and supporters who were seeking, in universities, unities to hold the social order together. With its dozens of departments, its professional schools, museums, preparatory divisions, publishing houses, and extension services the modern university challenged the energies of the most aggressive administrator. Gothic architecture—early, late, or middle—emerged as a symbol of reassurance for some of the era's most anxious critics. Fostering the style within a research university emphasized, as Jean Block points out, its priestly function, its mediating role. But it served also to remind each school and sector of its subordinate place within the larger setting.

In the history of the University of Chicago the theme of mutual dependence would be surrounded by many presidents and deans, insisting that survival and prosperity requires that professional and disciplinary ambitions be subordinated to the goals of the University as a whole. The campus stamped its parts with a single impress. A Cambridge University vice-chancellor, visiting after World War I, termed Chicago "one of the most complete and uniform of all American universities," and found himself repeating the interpretation of the dramatic unities as Mr. Curdle explained them to Nicholas Nickleby, "a completeness—a kind of universal dovetailedness with regard to place and time—a sort of general oneness, if I may be allowed to use so strong an expression." Whether this unity resulted from the University "anticipating its own vastness," as the American journalist Julian Street put it about the same time, or simply reflected the conjunction of dream and opportunity, the result was to establish a strong sense of corporate self, within only a decade or two of the new foundation. The university of Chicago would never lose a sense of presence that gave it, even as a comparative newcomer, a special personality among the country's universities.

The two problems—connecting to the outer world and imposing some organizational ideal upon the inner structure—would be solved in various ways by colleges and universities in succeeding decades. Campuses expanding considerably in the 1950s, 1960s, and 1970s, would project different values and experiences. Chicago's Gothic campus presented only one approach, but that it exemplified. The survival of classic texts and a concern for the centrality and even fixity of form would, as it happened, become themes in the university's pedagogical and intellectual style during the twentieth century. The campus was receptive, of course. To other styles also. But when so much is anomalous about the landscape of learning, and when so many paradoxes and ironies mock the pretensions of founders and pioneers, it is reassuring to find some correspondences linking physical setting with human activity.

So far as monumentality and architectural decoration are concerned, this is a moment of reassessment. History has come, once again, to the rescue of revivalism, exposing the conceits supporting any effort to operate outside the need for adornment or temporal association. It is not clear how long this moment will last. But it provides the opportunity to reexamine the logic as well as the pieties of this older vocabulary.

Main Quadrangles, North

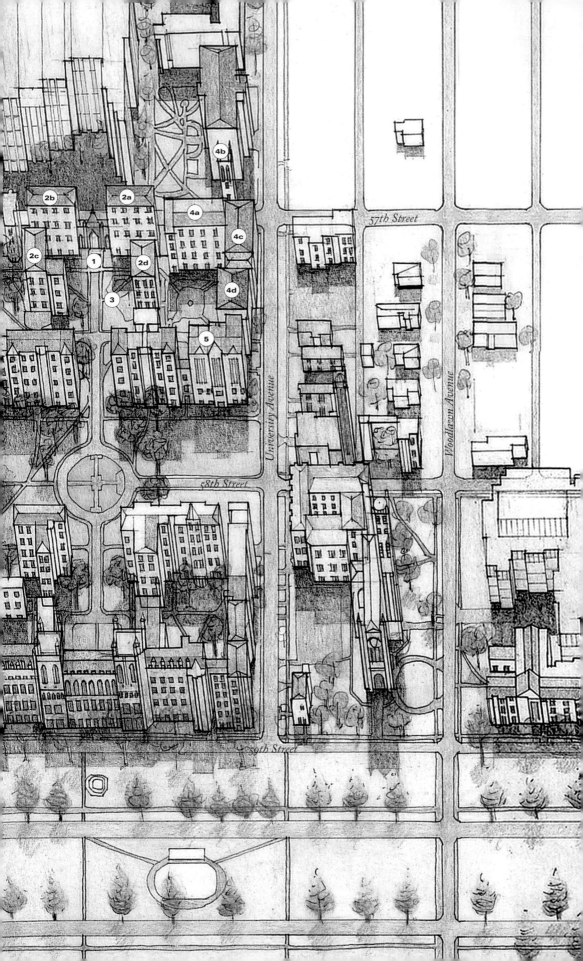

57th Street

58th Street

59th Street

University Avenue

Woodlawn Avenue

Of Griffins, Gargoyles, and the Gothic Revival

A stately griffin sits perched on the peak of Cobb Gate. Its appearance, with rippling muscles and powerful look, is well within the conventions of medieval ornament, but there is something unusual about this one. Perhaps it is the moustache, which seems not just fanciful but—appropriately, given the place—professorial. Architect Henry Ives Cobb (1859–1931) never recorded what inspired this figure or any of the other "grotesques" on his gate, but legends have been passed down about what he may have had in mind, which was certainly a whimsical, if not sarcastic, view of the solemn customs of the academic precincts within.

Cobb had reason to caricature the ironies of university life. When he designed Cobb Gate in 1900 and donated it to the client out of gratitude for a decade of work—he was on the ropes as university architect. He was suffering sharp, perhaps unjustified, reprimands for delay and inattention to interiors, particularly on the buildings around Hull Biological Laboratories nearby. Cobb had served as the university architect for a period of ten years; he had laid out the quadrangles, designed the earliest buildings on campus, and established a durable template for the campus—and had done so under budget constraints that might have defeated lesser architects. Still, he was fired shortly after designing Cobb Gate, replaced by what must have been regarded as a fancier and better connected firm from Boston, Shepley, Rutan and Coolidge.

Despite this unfortunate end to his tenure at the university, Cobb's legacy on the campus remains remarkable. When the trustees hired him in 1891, they were amateurs in architecture and knew only that the campus they were to establish should be different from the popular neoclassical style, which was on the ascent in America and would crescendo at Chicago's 1893 world's fair. While the fair would symbolize commerce, profit, and corporate success, the university saw itself as an enterprise of individuality, truth, and a passion for knowledge. With Cobb's guidance, the committee sought to express this in the architecture, opting for something that looked like their ideas of Oxford or Cambridge. Their resources were far from limitless, however. Cobb, a practical architect with roots in the Chicago School, gave them a version of Gothic revival on a budget, and what he accomplished was remarkable. His functional buildings with Gothic flourishes—oriels, arches, parapets, and traceries—bear only scant resemblance to the medieval models of old England, but they were assembled with restraint and taste and were quickly accepted as an architecture to which the university would become happily accustomed.

What we will see in this walk, and what we are likely to conclude from touring the university at large, is that Cobb's relatively simple Gothic buildings—purists would say they are hardly Gothic at all—were the right style for a time when the university had infinite needs but finite funds. The least you can say for Henry Ives Cobb is that he made the most with what little money he had. More aptly, he was responsible for a campus plan and an original architectural style that took on a life of its own for decades after he was gone.

1. Cobb Gate   *Henry Ives Cobb, 1900*

The gate named for the architect was Henry Ives Cobb's most personal design and also his swan song at the university. Cobb paid for it himself and gave it an extravagance that his fifteen other tightly budgeted buildings at the university could not afford. Built of Blue Bedford (Indiana) limestone, the gate has a red-tiled canopy overhead, echoing the pitched roofs on all of Cobb's buildings for the university, including the four around Hull Court, directly inside this ornate entry.

Cobb Gate is best known for the grotesques that inhabit the edge of its steep gable (duplicated on both sides). It is a vivid tableau, and students over the years have given the creatures an elaborate unwritten meaning. The most common version goes like this: At the base of the eaves, the

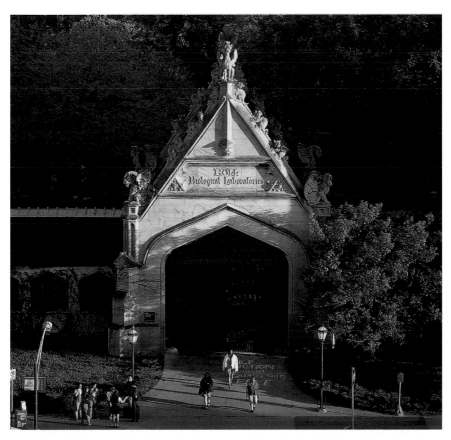

Cobb Gate

dragon-like concoctions with long necks and predatory expressions are admissions officers. First-year students who have just gotten through are depicted as skittish, rodent-like creatures, hanging on for dear life. Beyond them are second- and third-years—larger copies of the same species with increasingly confident grips (and increasingly snarling mien). The large griffin on top, metamorphosed into something not exactly beautiful but certainly stately, is enjoying the position of a forth-year upperclassman, basking briefly in his success before taking hypothetical flight.

Carved figures and stories that accompany them are not uncommon in Gothic architecture. In general they are meant to shock and surprise—from open-mouthed gargoyles that spew water to figures that caricature contemporary people. At Cobb Gate, it is hard not to think of the stone carver, laughing to himself as he carved the proud griffin whose command is secretly compromised by the fact that his muscular loins undeniably appear to be attached backwards to the rest of the body. What may pass unnoticed from the street would have humored the artisan and anyone else who noticed: an anatomically challenged power figure guarding a gate to, among other things, the great university's Department of Anatomy.

2. Hull Biological Laboratories

Zoology Building *Henry Ives Cobb, 1897*

Anatomy Building *Henry Ives Cobb, 1897*

Culver Hall *Henry Ives Cobb, 1897*

Erman Botany Building *Henry Ives Cobb, 1897*

Besides the humor that enhances Cobb Gate, its elaboration also serves to moderate the relative plainness of the four buildings around Hull Court. The simplicity of these buildings can be explained in at least two ways. One of them is cost. When Hull Biological Laboratories (all in the uniform material of Bedford limestone) were built in 1897, the six-year-old university's need for buildings was urgent, and no attainable amount of money would have satisfied all requirements. Zoology Building to the east of Cobb Gate and Anatomy Building to the west cost less than $100,000 each, low even by nineteenth-century standards.

The simplicity of the Hull laboratories can also be explained by Cobb's background. He was less a confirmed gothicist than a talented architect of his time and place, whose upbringing was in the "Chicago commercial style," also called the Chicago School, which was noted for originality and grace in rectangular, sparsely ornamented buildings. Zoology exhibits

OPPOSITE: *Cobb Gate, grotesques*

LEFT: *Zoology Building, entrance*
RIGHT: *Zoology Building, door detail*

this tendency in particular with large, carefully proportioned windows as the main feature of the four-story building. Its Gothic elements are most prominent in the roof line, with steep-pitched gables and decorative wrought iron work at the peak. Maybe Saul Bellow was intrigued by the building's simple grayness and muted Gothic spirit, for he used it in his novel *Herzog* (1964) as setting for Professor Moses Herzog to learn that his wife was betraying him with his best friend. (Witnessing this scene is a tubercular monkey, evidently a test subject in the laboratory, who provides poor Herzog with little relief and no solace.)

The Anatomy Building was built at the same time under the same conditions. Massed like Zoology to maintain balance, Anatomy's detailing is strikingly different, in obvious deference to the asymmetrical demands of the Gothic. Its more complicated ornament includes an arcade along the third and fourth floors with a course of pointed arches across the top. The

Zoology Building

LEFT: *Anatomy Building*
RIGHT: *Erman Botany Building, with Cobb Gate in foreground*

arcade has no traditional analog and is only vaguely "Gothic" in any classic sense. It may instead have been inspired by another Cobb design, the more elaborate Venetian-like arcade on the Michigan Avenue facade of the Chicago Athletic Association, completed the year before. That building was praised by a local newspaper as "a highly intelligent and artistic performance." Here, a similar detail element is scaled down and carved with simpler geometry to meet the demands of a client without the luxury of time or money.

The two buildings on the east and west side of the courtyard, Botany (later known as Erman) and Culver (also known as Physiology), completed the university's first proper quadrangle of the many that were planned. A gift from real estate magnate Helen Culver paid for these two buildings as well as for Zoology and Anatomy. (Hull Court is named in honor of her cousin Charles Hull—Hull House on Halsted Street had been his home—whose business she inherited after his death.) Helen Culver had no particular connection to the biological sciences, but she was, like many of the early donors, a practical commercial person and must have been attracted by the concrete nature of scientific research. This university, moreover, was careful to stress the noble and perhaps divine purpose of scientific pursuit. In the 1897 dedicatory exercises for the Hull laboratories, Miss Culver herself stated the view eloquently. "I have believed that moral evils would grow less as knowledge of their relation to physical life prevails— and that science, which is knowing, knowing the truth, is a foundation of pure religion."

In massing, Culver and Botany are identical but they have a substantially different collection of details. Botany's plain character is reinforced by a total lack of the gargoyles or other grotesques that are present (if spare) on other buildings of the Hull group. Why not on Botany? Some say it was the architect's fanciful desire to leave the plant life therein unmolested by animal life. What is clear is that the varied ornamentation of the two buildings appears motivated by the Gothic need to appear random, not obviously designed as a piece but assembled over the ennobling passage of time.

TOP: *Culver Hall*
BOTTOM: *Hull Gate*

Botany Pond with bridge

3. Botany Pond *Olmsted Brothers, c. 1901*

Another curious element of the Botany and Culver buildings is that both are without doors leading on to Hull Court; each has its main entrance in small quadrangles or courtyards on the opposite side. This lack of access to the courtyard goes unexplained except for the fact that Cobb consulted deeply with biology professor Robert Coulter regarding many elements of this complex. Among other things, Coulter was eager to create the small ecosystem of Botany Pond, a largely naturalistic water feature as part of Hull Court. One can imagine that busy entrances to buildings on either side would have created traffic patterns that might have compromised the viability of the pond.

Botany Pond was originally designed by the Olmsted Brothers who simultaneously laid out the open spaces of the quadrangles. It was subject to some neglect over the years; recently, it was carefully replanted with large exotic cultivars, which designers intended to appear primeval and critics have found "Flintstone-like." Botany Pond continues to serve as a peaceful haven for students, less so for baby geese that return every year despite the presence of predatory alley cats lying in wait.

Hutchinson Court, fountain

4. Tower Group

Hutchinson Commons   *Shepley, Rutan and Coolidge, 1903*

Mitchell Tower   *Shepley, Rutan and Coolidge, 1903*

Reynolds Club   *Shepley, Rutan and Coolidge, 1903*

Mandel Hall   *Shepley, Rutan and Coolidge, 1903*

Renovation   *Skidmore, Owings and Merrill, 1982*

A short breezeway or cloister connects Zoology and Botany on the far edge of Botany Pond. This provides a touch of intimacy on a campus that Cobb knew would quickly grow large. What he could not have known when he designed the cloister was that the passage through it, from Hull to Hutchinson Court, would come to represent a significant transition from one era of the university's architecture to another.

Many things changed in the ten years that separated the design of Cobb's original buildings on campus and that of the Tower Group by the Boston firm of Shepley, Rutan and Coolidge. Among them was the fact that John D. Rockefeller had become a true believer in the university's future and his original contribution of $600,000 was fast expanding to what would become $35 million. Other donors were coming forth as well, and in 1901, when Charles Coolidge became the principal architect of the university, his commission included amenities that would have seemed a luxury in the Cobb era: a well-equipped student commons and a landmark bell tower. Two years later, the Tower Group was completed, and the result was a far

Hutchinson Commons, dining room

different version of the Gothic revival than what Cobb had created in his time.

These buildings show a new delicacy, definitely a function of increased budgets but also the result of a more ambitious design, immediately evident as one passes through the cloister from Hull Court. This is not to diminish the importance of Cobb, whose scale, choice of materials, and many other elements are echoed in the later buildings. But even the physical approach to the Tower Group from Hull Court reflects a new subtlety: the passage appears to dead-end at an ivy-covered wall until the visitor reaches the wall and is drawn immediately to the right into a large, leafy courtyard. Pleasant surprises such as this were de rigueur in the refined architecture of eastern gothicists.

Coolidge shows here that he had a clear penchant for abundant references to Old England, a shift mandated no later than 1900 when trustee Charles Hutchinson traveled to Oxford with the Boston architect. "I am coming home with great ideas of what our future buildings should be," wrote Hutchinson to President Harper, "and only wish that we might begin all over again." At Oxford, Hutchinson had workmen take detailed measurements of various buildings both inside and out. The University of Chicago now had the money and the will to look ever so much more like the medieval university of the founders' imagination.

Among such limestone dreams, Hutchinson Commons was modeled after Oxford's Christ Church Hall (built in the mid-1500s), a classic example of the late–Gothic English Perpendicular. The commons project is also an excellent illustration of the revivalist principle of adapting details from the old but never copying it whole. This was a matter of design pride,

Hutchinson Commons, window with seals of Europe's great universities

perhaps, but also of function. Here, the architects modified their building with aisles on each side for practical contemporary needs—a kitchen on one side and a café on the other, both surmounted by fine parapets. The arrangement demonstrated the great strength of the Gothic style. It could be deconstructed and reassembled in many ways without compromising its nobility or charm.

The interior of Hutchinson, with its heavy beams and high clerestories, remains one of the more ennobling spaces of the university. Detailed with carved stone fireplaces and metalwork chandeliers and decorated with large paintings of university presidents and trustees, the design reflects an enduring love of honest craftsmanship, regarded as medieval architecture's gift to the modern world. Another message from the past was brought home in a story of the Prince of Wales's visit here in 1924. When told that the commons was modeled after Christ Church Hall, the prince deadpanned, "except we don't wash the windows." Possibly for that reason, or because of the expense of scaffolding, the building's windows were not washed until 1950, and then waited another two decades to be cleaned again.

Mitchell Tower represents another adaptation of an Oxford icon: Magdalen Tower, built in 1509. Here again, the design is changed for practical reasons and local use. The Chicago version rises fourteen feet shorter than the Oxonian one, the better to harmonize with other pieces of the university's increasingly intricate Gothic puzzle. And on top, the crocketed finials of the English building were replaced with octagonal turrets to echo the existing towers over Ryerson Laboratories across Hutchinson Court.

Like Magdalen, Mitchell Tower is home to ten "changing" bells that can carry simple tunes but in their most esoteric use are sounded in nonmusical sequences of mathematical precision. Early on, neighbors of the tower found the nightly practice a regular racket and had long ringing curtailed shortly after the bells were installed in 1908. A little later, Amos Alonzo Stagg, the university's legendary football coach, was favored with a short 9:50 p.m. rendition of the university's song "Alma Mater" to remind his athletes that bedtime was nigh. In recent decades, enthusiasts of "change ringing," as it is called, are occasionally indulged. The practice, which seems frankly more scientific than artistic, is also a physical ordeal, and ringers say they favor hours-long marathons wherein complex patterns induce, it is said, a kind of trance in the practitioners, and perhaps a kind of headache in close-by neighbors.

Mitchell Tower with Hutchinson Court in foreground

Reynolds Club, foyer

The Reynolds Club, whose exterior is visible mostly from University Avenue (due to the corner configuration of the Tower Group), was loosely based on another Oxford model, St. John's College. Perhaps because it was the group's least visible building from inside the courtyard, Reynolds is the least elaborate of the four, though three second-floor oriel windows along University Avenue suggest the importance, if not grandeur, of student activity spaces within.

Reynolds is noted mostly for the interior designs by Frederick Clay Bartlett, whose work and name recur in nearby Bartlett Commons, which was donated by the designer's father. Bartlett, an accomplished mural painter, was also a great proponent of the arts and crafts movement, and here he intentionally darkened the oak paneling to suggest venerable age; he ordered Stickley furniture, which survives in photographs and was then of the most "modern" style, harmonizing as it did with the medieval. The small theater on the third floor remains a warm and useful space with carved and disproportionately large beam work giving the space a singular presence. The brass seal on the lobby floor is regarded as the first appearance of the winged phoenix as symbol of the University of Chicago.

Mandel Hall, modeled after the great room of a private fourteenth-century country house in England, was much appreciated when built for its service as chapel and assembly hall (demonstrating, if nothing else, the ecclesiastical-secular blend of the university). The Chicago Symphony Orchestra gave many of its earliest performances in it. The building had a

OPPOSITE: *Reynolds Club, entrance*

LEFT: *Mandel Hall*
RIGHT: *Mandel Hall, balcony*

primary defect, however: the original architects were better at reproducing the visual elements of medieval Gothic than the acoustic ones (some, not all, medieval auditoriums transmit sound brilliantly). In the 1980s, the university resolved to bring Mandel's functionality up to its splendid medieval form and hired Skidmore, Owings and Merrill (SOM) to renovate the space. The firm's knowledge of modern acoustical science proved exemplary, and

Mandel Hall, stage

to attain perfect sound in an imperfect space, SOM placed flat panels, called "clouds," hanging from the ceiling. These elements serve acoustical function more than optical form, certainly, but the Gothic revival interior remains both evocative and useful.

Even before its renovation, Mandel had long played its part in university theatrics. The famous Blackfriars annual musical was performed here. And significantly, it also served as backdrop for the early Court Theater when it staged outdoor summer performances in Hutchinson Court. Vivid in the memory of many Hyde Parkers is a 1963 production of *King Lear*. Director Robert Benedetti "found Court's setting outside Mandel Hall to be especially advantageous in emphasizing Lear's mythic origins dating back to the time of great barbarism," as the *University of Chicago Magazine* wrote in 1981.

5. Eckhart Hall *Charles Z. Klauder, 1930*

Eckhart Hall

The completion of Eckhart represented a late and highly skillful phase of Chicago Gothic. It also served to complete Hutchinson Court some years after it was begun by Cobb and largely realized by Coolidge. The building, donated by Bernard A. Eckhart, industrialist and civic official (Eckhart Park on the near West Side is named for him), also solved a problem for the mathematics department, which had been sharing crowded space in Ryerson and Cobb halls.

The architect commissioned for the new home of the mathematics department was Charles Z. Klauder of Philadelphia, the most distinguished specialist in the Gothic revival then active, with work spanning a number of universities, from Princeton University to the University of Colorado. Klauder was also the architect for the Cathedral of Learning, academia's then-tallest (and still most-decorative) high-rise, at the University of Pittsburgh.

Eckhart Hall has elaborate exhibitions of carved stone in the best English Perpendicular, with arched entrances and decorated windows. Its original iconography includes a schematic of the Pythagorean theorem over an arch on Hutchinson Court. As the building's ornament emerges naturally from broad flat planes of its mass, we discern an undeniable modernity in Klauder's Gothic, in the manner of Bertram Goodhue's Rockefeller Chapel built a few years earlier.

Main Quadrangles, Center, Southwest

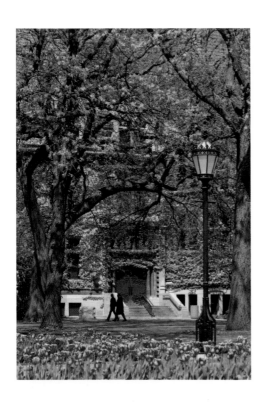

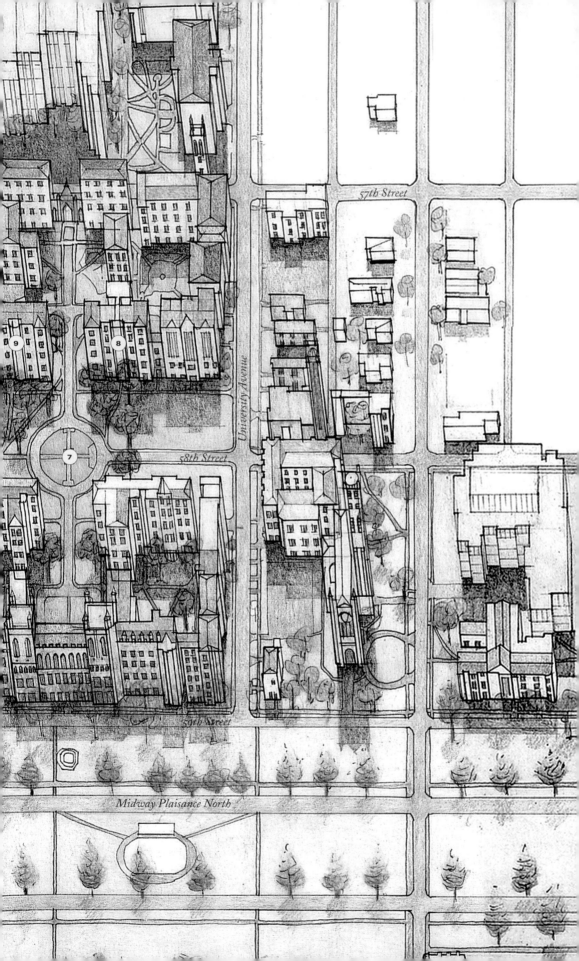

The Roots of "Chicago Gothic"

Standing in the middle of the university's Main Quadrangles, it is hard to imagine an American setting with a more medieval feel than this one. Not that the nation lacks for college campuses in a similar style. Princeton and West Point built their Gothic romances in the late 1800s. Yale did the same as the fashion for English Perpendicular overtook New Haven's earlier penchant for Georgian colonial. Stanford, too, got its own version, a kind of Spanish Gothic. But the University of Chicago has a cohesive quality, stage-like yet authentic, that escapes most other large schools.

One of the many reasons for its architectural success may be that the university was founded not with modest ambitions and hopes for a gradual growth but as a major institution based on large ideas and in full expectation that it would be a great center of learning. Thus, an elaborate academic plan was quickly published and largely executed over time; simultaneously, an architectural road map was established and followed to a great extent for several subsequent decades. The result is remarkable architectural continuity, to say nothing of the university's academic success.

Nor can it be ignored that the setting was Chicago, which was, in the late nineteenth and early twentieth centuries, the undisputed center of American architecture. All over Chicago, designers, builders, and clients were eager to demonstrate that this city really was an "Athens by the Lake," as it was sometimes called by local journalists. Chicagoans read and wrote endlessly about what constituted architectural truth. And as they sought answers in the highly popular writings of John Ruskin and William Morris, many landed on the principles of the medieval past.

The university's destiny was Gothic, to be sure, but getting there was hardly a straight path. Henry Ives Cobb had an eclectic portfolio, and his first scheme for the university seemed like a safe if uninspired choice: a broad rectangular building with the symmetry of a beaux-arts palace, decorated with the Romanesque stone arches that were fashionable in the 1880s. But the trustees were not convinced, and it subsequently came out that what they really had in mind were the five-hundred-year-old campuses of Oxford and Cambridge. They finally wrote to Cobb that they should wish something "in the very latest English Gothic."

By mid-1891, Cobb was working on Gothic schemes that had an enclosed, almost cloistered ambiance of courtyards and a veritable maze of interconnected buildings with pointed arches and battlements. The architect produced at least two comprehensive plans that year, and the last one was endorsed by everyone involved. On a four-block site were seven quadrangles—three on each side of a central court with a fine chapel at one end and a stately administration building on the other. This looked like a university.

It was something of a pipe dream, in fact. Anyone who could read renderings could tell that the chapel and the administration building were too large for the rest. Other structures were out of scale too. But impracticalities could not diminish the impressiveness of Cobb's plan or the architect's apparent understanding of what the trustees wanted. Within the orderly quadrangles, which would be laid out immediately, buildings appeared random and picturesque. Roof lines were jagged, carved stone ubiquitous. Perhaps most important, however, was that Cobb's plan could be executed over time and by a variety of architects. Cobb's pencil was fanciful, and many well loved buildings of the next ten years were his own designs. But the fundamental choices he made in 1891 survived his tenure as university architect and turned out to be a road map that would guide campus building for the next fifty years.

6. Cobb Hall *Henry Ives Cobb, 1892*

The university's first building, which included a "general recitation" hall, classrooms, offices, and even a chapel, was named not for the architect but for a benefactor, Silas Cobb, who provided the funds for it. Cobb Hall is not Cobb's best design, but it was the largest of his sixteen buildings on campus and also the most expensive at $220,000. Most importantly, it set the tone in terms of style and materials for the architect's subsequent work and for the work of others who came after he had moved on.

Cobb chose Blue Bedford limestone from southern Indiana as the building material for Cobb Hall. (Bedford was not then but would become a highly desirable building stone, supplying the Empire State Building and the Pentagon in later years.) There was discussion of brick, but that was dismissed as unsuitable for the tone the trustees had in mind. Cobb may also have considered the Lemont limestone from southwest Cook and Will counties, popular at the time because it was lighter in color. His choice of Bedford turned out to be a happy one, though, as the stone was plentiful, durable, and well-suited to the desirable illusion that the university was an ancient one.

Cobb Hall is filled with Gothic imagery and workmanship, yet it reveals as much about Cobb's background in the Chicago School as it shows of his skill in Gothic revival. Its plan is essentially as simple as a downtown office building: a rectangular block with outer bearing walls and interior iron supports, the latter carrying sufficient load to enable wide windows and large open spaces inside. Yet the Chicago-style simplicity, however important to the result, is concealed in ornament, with oriel corners, high-peaked gables, and finials overhead giving the university's first building an Oxonian feel.

Another important feature of Cobb Hall would be continued in many buildings in the coming decades and would deeply affect the character of the campus at large. The building was designed to face inward, with

its main entrance on the courtyard. This left Cobb's outside wall on Ellis Avenue mostly plain and even fortress-like, creating the impression that the university was a private precinct, apart from the hurly-burly of the world outside. This was precisely the idea that the architect intended, though it was regarded as regrettable years later when efforts were made to reduce social barriers between town and gown.

If there was another unsatisfactory aspect of Cobb Hall, it was the rooms inside, which were cold and utilitarian. Julius Lewis, who wrote a biography of Cobb as his student thesis in 1951, described the interior spaces as "grotesque," an exaggeration perhaps, but they were certainly cut of different cloth than the exterior. In 1965, when the School of Social Service Administration building south of the Midway was completed and its faculty could properly vacate its previous offices in Cobb Hall, the building began a major renovation, one of many guttings in that decade. After an interior makeover, Cobb was turned over entirely to the humanities and social sciences as a lecture hall, and the home of the Renaissance Society Art Gallery.

7. Main Quadrangle *Principal layout by Olmsted Brothers, 1902*

The first landscape architect to apply himself to Cobb's university plan was O. C. Simonds shortly after 1891. Simonds's work showed elements of the Prairie School in that he sought broad landscapes that emphasized nat- ural landforms. In fact, there were few indigenous forms on the mostly windswept flats of Hyde Park, but Simonds designed and began to execute a system of winding paths and a variety of native plants. In addition, Judge Daniel Shorey, a trustee, encouraged the planting of hardwoods, notably black oaks, which have done well in the sandy soil of Hyde Park.

Simonds's naturalism was short-lived, however, as the trustees replaced him with designers of a more rectilinear plan. In 1901 the Boston- based Olmsted Brothers provided a largely formal campus layout (despite the firm's forebear, Frederick Law Olmsted, who created grandiose parklike settings, such as Jackson and Washington parks nearby). Olmsted's son and stepson (Frederick, Jr., 1870–1957, and John C. Olmsted, 1852–1920) designed roadways, walkways, and plantings that faithfully followed Cobb's plan of main and subsidiary quadrangles.

The third notable landscape designer to have a hand in the Main Quadrangle as well as other gardens and courtyards around campus was Beatrix Jones Farrand. Her main objective when she arrived in 1929 was to exile cars from campus with a system of greenswards, diagonal walks, and leafy parkways. The community revolted against the auto ban, however,

OPPOSITE: *Cobb Hall*

and Farrand's main contribution was a softening of the limestone masses of the architecture with a new abundance of woody plants and ornamental trees—the burning bush was a favorite. Today's fashion for native and naturalized perennials in many beds around campus can also be traced back to Farrand's rigor in selecting plants for color, habit, and hardiness.

8. Ryerson Physical Laboratory *Henry Ives Cobb, 1894*

Ryerson Annex *Shepley, Rutan and Coolidge, 1913*

On the north edge of the Main Quadrangle stand two of Cobb's more mature buildings. In Ryerson and Kent, Cobb shows himself to be more relaxed and elaborate than in other designs, a function of more generous budgets. With the relative luxury of increased funding (Ryerson was donated by Martin Ryerson in memory of his father), the architect clearly enjoyed designing grander exteriors. Ryerson's floor plan is conventional, almost classical, with a central hall and block at each end. The exterior treatment, on the other hand, exhibits a dreamy Gothic fantasy: complicated solids and voids on the surface, with balconies, gables, and a crocketed roof line. As usual in Cobb's buildings, the main entrance is the most elaborate part, conspicuously buttressed on both sides; the resulting fortress-like feel is reinforced with crenellations atop. Adjacent is an octagonal tower with slit windows corresponding to a spiral staircase running up the inside.

At Ryerson's dedication, President Harper called it the most beautiful university building in the world. What was less discussed at the time and little understood were features designed for the delicate scientific work inside. The building had extra-heavy foundations to minimize vibration, and basement laboratories in particular were lined with thick cork for maximum insulation and moisture control. One of Ryerson's earliest denizens was physicist Albert Michelson, the first Nobel laureate among many at this university. Michelson was honored in 1907 for his measurement of the speed of light.

An annex to Ryerson was designed by Shepley, Rutan and Coolidge and built in 1913. While the treatment is restrained and sympathetic to Cobb's simple, double-hung fenestration, the later design includes mullioned windows and noticeably richer ornamentation. In 1983, higher-than-normal radiation levels in the building led to a complete renovation to make it radiation-free, after which the remaining elements of the physics department moved to Kersten Hall across Ellis Avenue, and the Department of Computer Science moved in.

Ryerson Physical Laboratory

9. **Kent Chemical Laboratory** *Henry Ives Cobb, 1894*

Kent, built in the same year as Ryerson, again demonstrates Cobb's personal skill in detail and ornament when there was enough money for such luxuries. This laboratory is similar in plan to Ryerson, with a central section and two wings of equal size. Yet the Gothic preference for irregularity demanded that Kent appear asymmetrical in elevation and remain distinct from Ryerson. Here, Cobb added a wide octagonal stair tower capped with a steep conical roof.

Kent's octagonal form is repeated in large scale in a wing behind the main section of the laboratory building. Kent Lecture Hall was once the largest auditorium of the university (before Mandel Hall was completed). Here non-scientific as well as scientific assemblies took place, such as a special convocation that awarded an honorary degree to President McKinley and cornerstone ceremonies for the Law School, which included President Theodore Roosevelt.

The Kent laboratory was built with a donation from Chicago businessman Sidney Kent, whose initial gift of $150,000 was the first to be

LEFT: *Kent Lecture Hall*
RIGHT: *George Herbert Jones Laboratory with Kent Chemical Laboratory in background*

applied to a goal of $1 million to match a challenge grant from Marshall Field. Kent was a grain speculator, not a scientist, but he was impressed by President Harper's insistence that the world was being transformed by science. "A century ago, there really was no science," said the president at Kent's dedication. But by the time the university was founded, its study had grown to include "everything from God himself to the most insignificant atom of his creation."

In the 1970s the building served as the office of the *Bulletin of the Atomic Scientists*, known largely for its dissent against the nuclear arms build-up. The magazine is particularly famous for its cover graphics with a clock designed by the noted artist Martyl Langsdorf; its minute hand moves back or forward toward midnight depending upon the planet's presumed closeness to nuclear disaster at that moment.

In 1983 the building was stripped to its limestone walls and decontaminated in a renovation for undergraduate classrooms and laboratories in chemistry. Recovered was most of the best of its wood detailing as well as a Lorado Taft bronze relief of the donor and the ornate strapping on the front door.

OPPOSITE: *Kent Chemical Laboratory*

C–Bench

10. C-Bench *Charles Z. Klauder, 1930*

Opposite the front door of Cobb Hall, the C-Bench is a reminder of the kind of traditions that once obsessed American collegians. Given by the Class of 1903, it was for the exclusive use of athletic lettermen (and the girls that they were kissing). Segregation of this sort was abolished (or it simply faded away) after World War II when athletes lost a measure of their prestige on campus. In the pavement in front of the bench is embedded a keystone from Douglas Hall at the original University of Chicago. Another notable feature is that the bench constitutes something of a parabolic chamber that amplifies whispers in unexpected ways.

11. Former Residence Halls

Gates-Blake Hall *Henry Ives Cobb, 1892*

Goodspeed Hall *Henry Ives Cobb, 1892*

The Bedford limestone buildings along the edge of the Southwest Quadrangle employ restrained Gothic details that tie them aesthetically to Cobb Hall. Gates and Blake halls, now considered a single building, and Goodspeed Hall feature oriels along their facades and gables along the roof line that are signs of the Chicago Gothic vocabulary in what are otherwise modest buildings. Blake was built a few months after Cobb Hall as a dormitory for graduate students. Goodspeed and Gates came immediately after and housed divinity students, most of them preparing for the ministry. Prior to construction, Board Secretary Thomas Goodspeed, himself a minister, had suggested that future preachers ought to be housed with other

Gates–Blake Hall

students, but President Harper preferred to have them separate, and his will was done.

These three buildings, which blend the simple massing of the Chicago School with the picturesque detailing of the Gothic, have proven highly versatile. Goodspeed Hall was converted to serve the art department in 1937 and was turned over to the music department in 1981 when the classics reading room in another adjacent building was made into a recital room. Gates-Blake was converted to offices in 1960 when its halls were connected to corresponding office and classroom space in Cobb Hall.

Fulton Recital Hall in Goodspeed Hall

Main Quadrangles, South

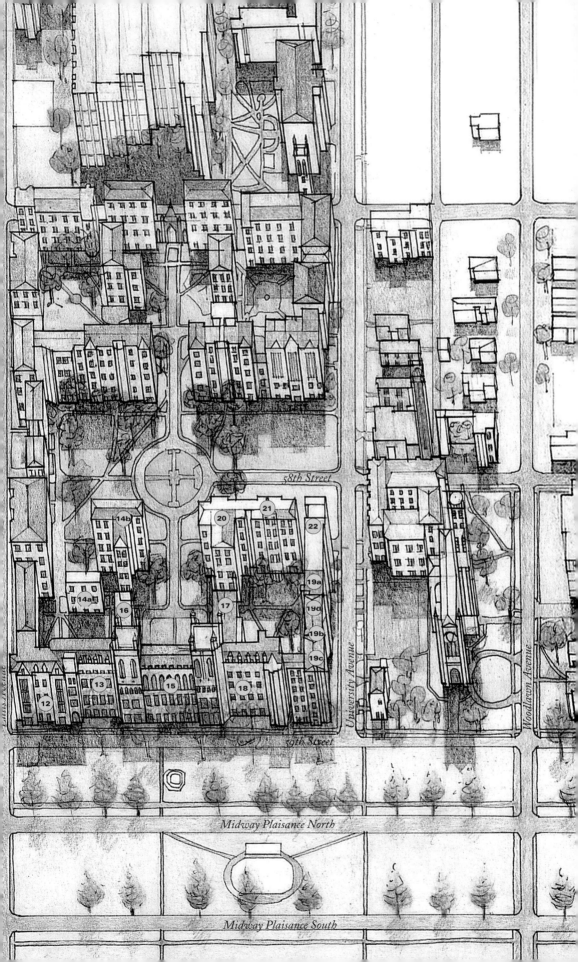

Growth of the Gothic Campus

The Southwest Quadrangle marks another transition from the Cobbian Gothic of the early university to the more elaborate versions that came later. Witness for instance Cobb's Goodspeed Hall (1892) connected to the Classics Building (1915) designed by Shepley, Rutan and Coolidge. The conjunction of these two buildings is not violent or overly conspicuous, due largely to the grayish Bedford stone used in both. Other harmonies tie these two buildings together as well, but their differences are also striking and significant. Cobb's building, like many of his designs, has a simplicity that one could call primitive; the work of the Shepley firm is richer in many ways, due in part to increased building budgets.

Shepley, Rutan and Coolidge arrived in 1901 just as the university's financial ship was coming in, with Rockefeller's contributions greatest among many increasing donations to the university. Comparing Goodspeed and Classics, consider the cost: While Goodspeed cost less than $60,000, Classics cost more that $150,000. If the differences between the two are not utterly obvious, it is a credit to Coolidge's restraint but also to Cobb's ability to make the most with the money he had.

In fact, the Boston firm of Shepley, Rutan and Coolidge was a larger and more "corporate" office than Cobb's firm, which was managed largely by the owner. The new campus architects had already risen to one of the leading practices in the nation at the time. In an age when wealthy eclecticism was the order of the day, the Boston architects had a remarkable grasp of how to blend historical imagery and current needs. Shepley, Rutan and Coolidge came to Chicago with enormous prestige, largely as direct successors to the practice of Henry Hobson Richardson. The nineteenth century's most pivotal architect, Richardson had freed himself more than anyone else to date from historical formulae. His Trinity Church in Boston and Glessner House in Chicago, modeled after the medieval Romanesque, had been hailed as proudly, if not exactly indigenously, American. Richardson used rusticated stone, massive arches, and open-plan interiors to achieve what American architects had long sought: freedom from strict historicism, which for most of the nineteenth century meant adherence to the beaux-arts classical and to a lesser extent the Gothic revival.

Richardson taught his protégés well, though not long after his death in 1886, European models came back in vogue in America. The arguable cause was Chicago's own Columbian Exposition, a beaux-arts extravaganza conducted a stone's throw away from the university. Suddenly classicism was the rage, and the Shepley firm kept up, especially in Chicago with the Art Institute (1893) and the Chicago Public Library (1897), both elaborately classical in design. Predictably, Chicago architects complained bitterly when their library went to an East Coast firm. This showed provincialism, perhaps, but they were certainly sorry they had mentioned it at all when Shepley,

Rutan and Coolidge decided that the solution was to open a Chicago office. They would win a great deal more local work in the next two decades, including the University of Chicago, where the firm and its successors designed fourteen buildings.

It was not too surprising that Shepley, Rutan and Coolidge won the commission as university architects in 1901. Charles Coolidge had grown friendly with Charles Hutchinson, trustee of both the university and the Art Institute. In 1900 Coolidge and Hutchinson visited Oxford together, ostensibly to make plans for the latter's donation of Hutchinson Commons but in a more general way contemplating the next phase of building at the university. About to celebrate its decennial, the university was now richer, as Rockefeller had been sufficiently pleased with progress to increase his stake, now contributing money for more buildings as well as land. (Rockefeller and Marshall Field bought and donated all available real estate on both sides of the Midway.)

With more resources and space, the university and Coolidge (who assumed the lead in his firm's relationship with the university) were able to realize whole new sections of a growing campus. Most elaborately, a humanities and social science complex would be constructed around the south quadrangles. Its centerpiece would be a marvelous and much-needed library.

Cobb's exclusion from these developments may seem unfair or sad in retrospect, though he remained busy primarily in Washington, D.C. and New York. It is undeniable that his template for Chicago Gothic guided Charles Coolidge in many ways, and that the latter's firm designed many buildings that are modeled after Oxbridge originals but are also true to the courtyards, materials, and general style established by Cobb. To their credit, Shepley, Rutan and Coolidge—and later a Chicago-based successor, Coolidge and Hodgdon—exercised a delicate touch in these designs, which were highly ornamental and well suited to the ambitious needs of the decade-old university.

12.   Classics Building   *Shepley, Rutan and Coolidge, 1915*

Stone carving on Classics Building

Classics was built with a donation from Elizabeth Green Kelly, who asked that the building also be known as the Hiram Kelly Memorial for her late husband. Dr. Kelly's name is carved over the north door, a conventional honorific. More surprising is the nature and abundance of sculptural ornament on the building. Much of it is of identifiable figures from the classical world, including the heads of Homer, Cicero, Socrates, Plato, and other classical thinkers carved into the corbels of door and window arches.

By this time, the building's architects had broadened the university's taste in stone carving beyond the standard tracery and crockets. Now the Coolidge firm was commonly creating symbolic ornament specific to each building. This was not new in Gothic architecture and was considered a virtue of the style—the ability to add any kind of figure, even contemporary portraiture, to a picturesque work of architecture. It also reflected expense, as each of these unique figures was modeled in clay, cast in plaster, then carved (sometimes on-site, sometimes in local workshops) with the help of a device that was part pantograph and part measuring caliper.

Expense or no, appropriate symbolism was taken seriously in this period, and official committees including trustees were charged with determining the carved repertoire for each building. Here at Classics, we witness a particular richness. One of the fabled Labors of Hercules (presumably the capture of Cerberus, though this hound has two heads instead of the legendary three) is illustrated under several oriel windows. On the cornice are figures from Aesop's *Fables*.

The windows in Classics—some of the narrow lancet type and others with carved mullions and traceried arches—reflect the increasingly refined Gothic style on campus in this period. These details can be described as English Perpendicular, and they correspond to other Shepley, Rutan and Coolidge work nearby, such as Harper Library two doors east. Yet the building's pitched roof, Tudor gables, and other "domestic" elements blend gracefully with Cobb's modest Goodspeed Hall (1892) to the west.

OPPOSITE: *Classics Building*

TOP: *Wieboldt Hall, detail*
BOTTOM: *Wieboldt Hall*

Commemorative plaque

Wieboldt, funded with a gift from the retail baron whose stores survived into the 1970s, was built to house the Department of Modern Languages. Completed more than a decade after Classics, which is on its west flank, the building incorporates an arched passage, one of only two walkways, both narrow, that connect the quadrangles to the Midway. Inside the passage on the wall, the architects made place for a small commemoration of the first University of Chicago, a metal engraving and piece of light limestone from the remains of Douglas Hall, the old school's main building, designed by W. W. Boyington.

On the Midway side of Wieboldt, a castellated tower and parapet may be another echo of old Douglas Hall. The design also features carvings of a few of the greats of Western literature: Dante, Chaucer, Shakespeare, Molière, Ibsen, and Emerson, among others.

14. Theology Group

Bond Chapel *Coolidge and Hodgdon, 1926*

Swift Hall (Divinity School) *Coolidge and Hodgdon, 1926*

A glance north reveals a traceried cloister that beckons the visitor forth. Drawing closer one reaches, almost by surprise, the entrance of Bond Chapel. This approach employs the subtle manipulation of space that the Gothic often shared with modernism—something we will encounter frequently in these quadrangles but never more dramatically than here.

The cloister connects Bond Chapel to Swift Hall (the Divinity School), both designed by Coolidge and Hodgdon, spun off from Shepley, Rutan and Coolidge earlier in the 1920s. By this time, modernism was in the air, and we see its influence, particularly in Swift. The small, jewel-like chapel, on the other hand, is drenched in Gothic symbolism and mystery. The recessed entrance, far more ornate and dramatic than its size might call for, is quite a performance with empty niches to either side, an arcade above the door, and a large mullioned window with decorative tracery at the peak.

Bond Chapel

Bond's design and iconography reaches well back to ancient Christianity, but at the 1926 dedication ceremony, Shailer Matthews, Dean of the Divinity School stressed the university's belief in modern learning. "Religion is an experiment by which we test the permanent meaning of our own souls," he said. In the earlier cornerstone address, he stated that religion must not count "ecclesiastical authority more precious than facts." Despite the university's modern views of religion, the exterior of the chapel is redolent of a Manichaean universe, with grotesques and other venal figures populating the cornice. The west wall is occupied by a tableau of Adam and Eve, with the snake and apple, though the story's doleful message is moderated by a fair population of angels and other godly figures that are also carved into the rich limestone ornament. Inside, the timber ceiling reflects the loving handwork that architects at this time associated with spiritual uplift. At the altar, the "urn of memory," symbolic of the ashes of material existence, is carved with a Byzantine foliate design that appears to grow lushly from the contents within. The liveliness of this ornament recalls, ironically perhaps, architecture's great modern prophet, Louis Sullivan.

That Bond was conceived as an essentially conservative work is confirmed by the chancel window by Charles J. Connick, the leading church glass artist of the time. Connick's reputation outstripped even that of John

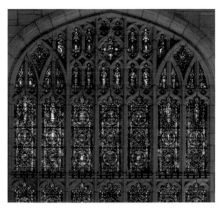

LEFT: *Bond Chapel, window*
RIGHT: *Swift Hall, lecture hall ceiling*

Comfort Tiffany, whose more "modern" opalescent windows might easily have overwhelmed this small space. Connick's window, donated by Thomas Goodspeed (who had married a daughter of radiator magnate Joseph Bond) is more traditional; it is separated into lancets, each one of which contains an icon of biblical symbology, including Disciples, Apostles, and Evangelists.

Swift Hall, the seat of the Divinity School, is connected physically (by the cloister) and functionally to Bond Chapel. Yet, unlike Bond, Swift was more clearly influenced by the modern tendency to simplify even Gothic forms. Wide planes of clear limestone exhibit a taste for the linear

Swift Hall

simplicity of the twentieth century. In general the solids are flatter and the voids shallower than in earlier buildings associated with Charles Coolidge. Yet latter-day plainness did not displace a love for fancy carving as the traceried windows among other Gothic detail in Swift show.

While Swift's exterior has few purely symbolic touches, the interior has abundant sculptural elements that render this building its unique character. On the first floor, the lobby features three commemorative tablets by Leonard Crunelle, Lorado Taft's most accomplished protégé, including a portrait of William Rainey Harper, who taught at the Baptist Theological Seminary, precursor to this Divinity School, before the university was founded. On the second floor, the timbered ceiling of the lecture hall, originally the library, is lovingly carved with oak figures, including angels bearing books—"divine messengers" as they are called here.

15. William Rainey Harper Memorial Library
Shepley, Rutan and Coolidge, 1912

The purchase of nearly all property lining the Midway in the 1920s enabled university planners to devote the South Quadrangle almost entirely to humanities and social sciences, with the Harper Memorial Library as centerpiece. Credit for this thoughtful plan goes to Charles Coolidge, whose foresight was responsible for the library's great hall and a network of departmental reading rooms in adjacent and nearby buildings, all connected by corridors and bridges. (The harmony between central and

Harper Memorial Library, north entrance

TOP: *Harper Memorial Library with statue of Linnaeus in foreground*
BOTTOM: *Harper Memorial Library, reading room*

satellite libraries has not been equaled since the main library was moved to Regenstein in the 1970s.)

In 1906, shortly after the premature death of President Harper, John D. Rockefeller, Jr. wrote to Martin Ryerson, president of the Board of Trustees, expressing an interest in building a library to commemorate the great educator and offering three dollars for every one dollar otherwise raised. Planning proceeded apace for a building that would cost more than $800,000 and be sited to anchor the principal north-south axis of the quadrangle complex. A door on the south was one of the first on campus to face outward—gates and not doors were still regarded as the proper way to get in from outside—but the main entrance to the library is on stately Harper Court.

While Chicago-born steel-frame construction had been used successfully for most buildings on campus, the architects here attempted to save money by using the relatively new construction technique of reinforced concrete. They regretted this experiment part way through, however, when the West Tower collapsed for reasons that were never entirely determined. It may have been the weight of a derrick, or sabotage connected to a workers' strike at the time, as Ryerson suspected. In any case, steel girders were added to the support of the West Tower, though not the East, where the placement of furniture and books by professors in their offices was frequently controlled by maintenance people (until a later renovation brought everything up to code). By design, the major load of library books was planned for stacks in the lower level of the building.

Harper's ornament was wrought with flourish and combines many elements of ancient models that the university held dear. The library's West Tower bears resemblance to King's College in Cambridge while the East Tower appears inspired by Christ Church Hall. Why dissimilar towers in an otherwise symmetrical scheme? Early university lore holds that the West Tower appears ecclesiastical, the East Tower military in character, and the pairing symbolized the union of religion and secular government. Later it was said that the dissimilarities signified the separation of church and state. Such was the flexibility of Gothic symbolism, which suited the times no matter what the prevailing winds.

The great reading room, which still houses books in the arts and humanities, must be classed as one of the striking rooms of the university; its dramatic features include deep-set perpendicular windows, groined vaults, and prolific heraldry. The corbels end with printer's marks (a convention previously used on Chicago's printer's row) and the shields of universities around the world, including the University of Chicago coat of arms. The phoenix of its design is sometimes said to symbolize the rebirth of the first University of Chicago—a valid image judging from the stately library that survives one hundred years later.

LEFT: *Haskell Hall*
RIGHT: *Haskell Hall, entrance*

16. Haskell Hall *Henry Ives Cobb, 1896*

Commenting on Haskell Hall in correspondence while he designed it, Cobb said that he "felt it unnecessary to make the building at all ornate in its out-line...the most important part of the building will in the future be the close view of the main entrance, which I have endeavored to make attractive." Haskell Hall was an "Oriental" museum, built partly with a donation from Mrs. Frederick Haskell, who was induced by her pastor to help create a place where the roots of religion could be investigated. The building became among other things a hall for collections accumulated by James Henry Breasted, a professor and author of Near Eastern history and archae-ology. As a museum that mounted public exhibits, Haskell required the large spaces and abundant light needed for such use, elements of the Chicago commercial style that had been overshadowed on this campus and elsewhere in the city, but not forgotten.

Despite Cobb's avowed effort to keep it simple, Haskell's facade on Harper Court is a thing of exotic beauty, with two bays beneath broad Tudor arches on either side of the entry and oriental-looking ogee arches over windows at each end. The window above the front door is an elaborate affair with flamboyant tracery that appears vaguely Byzantine, appropriate for the predecessor of the Oriental Institute, which was established in 1931.

In the late 1970s, Haskell became the quarters of the anthropology department, and the adaptability of the Chicago Gothic was challenged when a three-story totem pole was installed in the atrium inside.

LEFT: *Stuart Hall, with East Tower of Harper Memorial Library in background*
RIGHT: *Stuart Hall, carving above entrance*

17. Stuart Hall *Shepley, Rutan and Coolidge, 1904*

Stuart Hall is another work of the firm that successfully "Oxbridgized" the Chicago campus with elaborate buildings recalling the ancient stones of Oxford and Cambridge. Initially called simply the Law School, its design was loosely inspired by King's College, Cambridge, most distinctively with the four crowned corner towers. Such grandeur was expected, as President Theodore Roosevelt helped lay the Law School's cornerstone in 1903. Inside it was and is praiseworthy for its timber-roof reading room, which preceded the construction of Harper Library and was then connected to the central library by an arched bridge to the south.

In 1959 when the Law School moved across the Midway, the building was turned over to the Graduate School of Business. Until 1978 it was known as Business East until it was rededicated to Harold Leonard Stuart, a securities dealer involved in the invention of competitive bidding for modern bond sales. It was Stuart's open interior layout that made the building equally suitable for both business and law at different points in the university's history. Now it awaits use primarily by the Division of Humanities after the Business School vacated it and moved to its modern palace on East Campus.

Social Science Research Building

18. Social Science Research Building
Coolidge and Hodgdon, 1929

One apparent motivation in the design for this building was to make it distinctly different from Wieboldt Hall, with which it is symmetrically sited and massed on the other side of Harper Library. The Social Science Building shows the same modernizing influence as Wieboldt, however, with broad planes and large windows—elements that hint at its construction of steel frame and limestone-cladding.

Despite the relative modernity of the design, the entrance on the north facade is decorated with carved reliefs of thinkers, including Gibbon the historian, Bentham the philosopher, and Boas the anthropologist. The building also features stone-carved iconography significant to the field: a ballot, a slide rule, even a mechanical adding machine. The porch arches extravagantly over a walkway that runs parallel to the building, giving the Southeast Quadrangle, also occupied by women's dormitories, an elegance that was deemed suitable for female students.

In the past the building was occupied by the economics department and housed some of the university's more notable scholars, including several Nobel Prize winners. Thorstein Veblen's office was here when he railed against "the leisure class" and "conspicuous consumption" early in the twentieth century. Paul Douglas, an economics professor who would become a U.S. Senator, was remembered for his teaching in the first-floor classroom with a large round table. "Douglas allegedly climbed upon the table, crawled across its dusty middle and questioned a student seated across from him," wrote economist Walter Y. Oi in an article for the *American Economist* entitled " View From the Midway."

19. Former Women's Residence Halls

Beecher Hall *Henry Ives Cobb, 1894*

Kelly Hall *Henry Ives Cobb, 1894*

Foster Hall *Henry Ives Cobb, 1894*

Green Hall *Henry Ives Cobb, 1899*

While the men were housed on the west side of the Main Quadrangle in Goodspeed and its neighboring dormitories, the women lived in this parallel row of buildings a full two blocks away on the east side. It should be noted that coeducation was never in question at the University of Chicago, nor in most major universities and colleges in the West, where women were recognized for their importance in settling the frontier.

Kelly and Beecher halls were funded by a gift from Mrs. Hiram Kelly, who later also gave the Classics Building, and Mrs. Jerome Beecher, sister of Silas Cobb (who gave Cobb Hall). In 1893 they were completed as relatively sober mirror images of each other. Later in 1893, Foster Hall went up in honor of Dr. John H. Foster, whose widow funded this building, which was closest to the epicenter of the world's fair on the Midway that year. Perhaps because of the festive goings-on just a few yards away, the hall is elaborately gargoyled and crocketed, and ribbed turrets high in the air appear almost celebratory.

Five years later, Mrs. Kelly gave the money for another dorm, Green Hall, which was sited between Kelly and Beecher, built in honor of her parents. With the exception of Foster, which seems designed to meet the festive standard of the fair just across Fifty-ninth Street, Cobb's Gothic is predictable in most ways. All entries are on courtyards; equally spaced windows on the exterior reflect mostly single-room accommodations inside; and crocketed gables were rendered with economy.

These buildings were actually designed and detailed by Cobb after he had a visit from a delegation of women faculty, which included a professor of "sanitary science and household management." The architect evidently received instructions regarding the necessity for ample parlors, privacy in living quarters, and good ventilation. Students complained, nevertheless, that accommodations were too small. In the 1950s, Beecher, Green, and Kelly became collectively the Psychology Building. Foster now serves as offices for the Committee on Social Thought and other departments of the Division of Social Sciences.

TOP: *Foster Hall*
BOTTOM: *Green Hall*

LEFT: *Rosenwald Hall, detail*
RIGHT: *Rosenwald Hall, carved door*

20. Rosenwald Hall *Holabird and Roche, 1915*

Gothic revival architects in the early twentieth century insisted that theirs was a "living" style that could be adapted to modern uses and the modern spirit. In many ways this proved true, especially as Gothic asymmetry proved useful to the university's architecture-by-addition mode, and its medievalism suited the philosophic preferences of the time. Still, there were those who objected to such historicism in a modern university; one of them was geologist Thomas Chamberlin, who was not wholly at one with "the ceremonials of medieval institutions . . . which are associated with an undeveloped stage of scholarship." Even so, Chamberlin was involved in determining what was the most appropriate symbolism to be displayed on Rosenwald Hall, which was built in the Gothic style—that was not negotiable—to house the geology and geography departments.

Carvings are everywhere on this building. Over the door are sculptures of students in scholarly robes, one holding a hammer and the other a theodolite, which geologists used to measure angles. Also over the entrance is an image of an old man with a globe apparently ruined by volcanoes and natural devastation; opposite is a young man with the earth regenerate. Elsewhere are stone heads of luminaries in the field: On the west elevation is Leonardo who was credited for his early understanding of

OPPOSITE: *Rosenwald Hall*

Rosenwald Hall, stone carving

fossils. On the south are less famous ones such as Newbery, Dawson, and Winchell, each important in "the diffusion of geologic thought in America," according to an official university publication at the time. On the east side of the building is Marco Polo, a pioneer geographer. Also represented are other heroes of the geologic record: the gastropod, brachiopod, crinoid, and others. Altogether, nineteen carvings embellish this nicely wrought Gothic building designed by Holabird and Roche, a Chicago School firm with an eclectic touch (City Hall and old Soldier Field are their work; later came the Board of Trade and the Palmolive Building).

Rosenwald was built with a gift of $250,000 from Sears, Roebuck president Julius Rosenwald, part of a series of bequests that he made on his fiftieth birthday. A 1917 article in *Architectural Record* states that Rosenwald Hall represented a "modern spirit" in university architecture. "While the exteriors reflect the influence of the fourteenth and fifteenth centuries," a critic wrote, "the interiors are better adapted to the practical uses for which they were intended." Holabird and Roche was a firm that prided itself first and foremost on functional planning of their buildings, and Rosenwald is no exception. The building was designed with seismic measuring devices resting on a column of concrete that ran more than sixty feet deep. Atop a graceful octagonal stair tower in the rear of Rosenwald was a variety of meteorological equipment that measured weather as part of an arrangement with the United States Weather Bureau.

In 1972 the Graduate School of Business made Rosenwald a part of its complex. Its carved-oak detailing inside and cinquefoil arched windows were meticulously restored at the time. The Business School has since moved out, and Rosenwald now houses the Department of College Admissions and the Department of Economics.

Walker Museum

21. Walker Museum *Henry Ives Cobb, 1893*

Walker Museum was built to exhibit natural history artifacts, evidence of the riches of nature that blessed the great Midwest, according to donor George Walker, more than any other place in the world. His contribution to the university would be an indispensable pedagogical tool for the time: a paleontological collection drawn from far and wide, many from the exhibits brought to Chicago for the Columbian Exposition. The exterior of this Cobbian Gothic building with its simple bays and large windows indicates spacious, well-lit interior spaces designed for museum use. The circular stair tower was essential so as to leave main interior volumes open for exhibition.

Shortly after the Walker Museum was completed, great pressure for space made the building the office headquarters of several departments, including geology, geography, and anthropology. Stories are that partitions crowded the otherwise open spaces. Later, when Rosenwald Hall was built next door, Walker assumed its proper role as a museum, although by the

1920s its collections were no longer used intensively in teaching. Many had been sent to the Field Museum, but prior to a 1980s renovation its remaining museum-like spaces still contained dinosaur fossils, fascinating even if they were mostly irrelevant to the building's main occupant at the time—anthropology.

In 1979 a famous building swap was executed when the Graduate School of Business proposed the trade of Haskell Hall for Walker. The school believed that Walker's contiguity with Rosenwald, which in turn is contiguous to Stuart, would create an optimal configuration for its purposes. Anthropology moved into Haskell, and the Business School renovated Walker and took occupancy in 1981. Some argued that changes made inside—gaining a floor by compressing the dramatic high ceilings of the old museum—demonstrated the flexibility of the Gothic style, ever adaptable. In fact, it was more a tribute to the wonders of steel frames and the eminent Chicago School, which created large open spaces that were easily recast as comfortable offices and classrooms. After the Business School moved into the new Hyde Park Center in 2004, Walker now serves as offices for the college, including the Office of College Aid, and of the Humanities Division.

22. Albert Pick Hall   *Ralph Rapson, 1971*

The site for this building was the last empty parcel on the old quadrangles, and the need for a "hall for international studies" was urgent at the time. Edward Levi, then president of the university, noted at the building's dedication that scholarly exchange had grown among international neighbors but not to a uniformly positive effect. "We are very much aware," he said, "that this cooperation has increased the powers of destruction." Levi insisted, however, that scholarship must not surrender. "The organized cruelty of this century makes clear that appreciation and acquaintanceship are insufficient. The close quarters of the world make it essential that we not only understand others, but also understand ourselves."

The Cold War was very much a backdrop, perhaps an unconscious one, to the architecture. Ralph Rapson declared himself intent on fitting in Albert Pick Hall as part of the university's venerable Gothic quadrangles. Time revealed something else, of course: mostly the brutalist sensibility that was prevalent when the hall was built. Sheer force was indeed the order of the day, in diplomacy as well as in the heavy limestone masses of Pick Hall.

Rapson was a noted modernist at the time who had designed the Guthrie Theater in Minneapolis and embassies in Sweden and Denmark. When he built Pick Hall, it was regarded as a sensitive modern accompaniment to the older buildings nearby. Lately it seems clumsy, however, and the metal-frame windows and ribbed mansard roof resemble the cheap fittings of too many modern claptraps. Nevertheless, there is a certain grace

Dialogo *by Virginio Ferrari*

to the tinted glass within the asymmetrically spaced lithic buttresses, and the day may come when its defects will rankle less and allow the architectural virtues of the building to show clearly through. A similar future may await the metal sculpture outside, entitled *Dialogo*, by Virginio Ferrari, whose meaning of "serenity out of strife" is wrought in abstract terms that may well be readable in decades to come. *Dialogo*'s main point of interest at present is that some believe it casts a shadow resembling a hammer and sickle.

East Campus

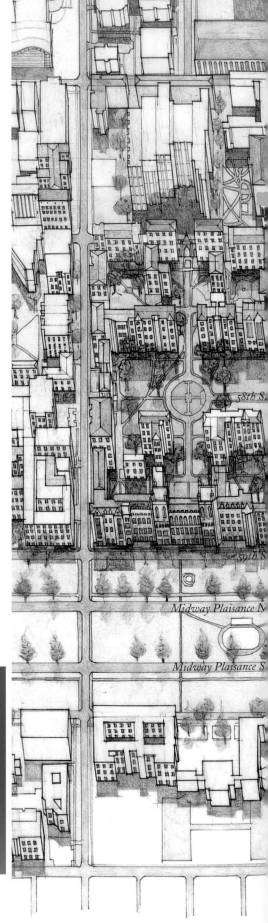

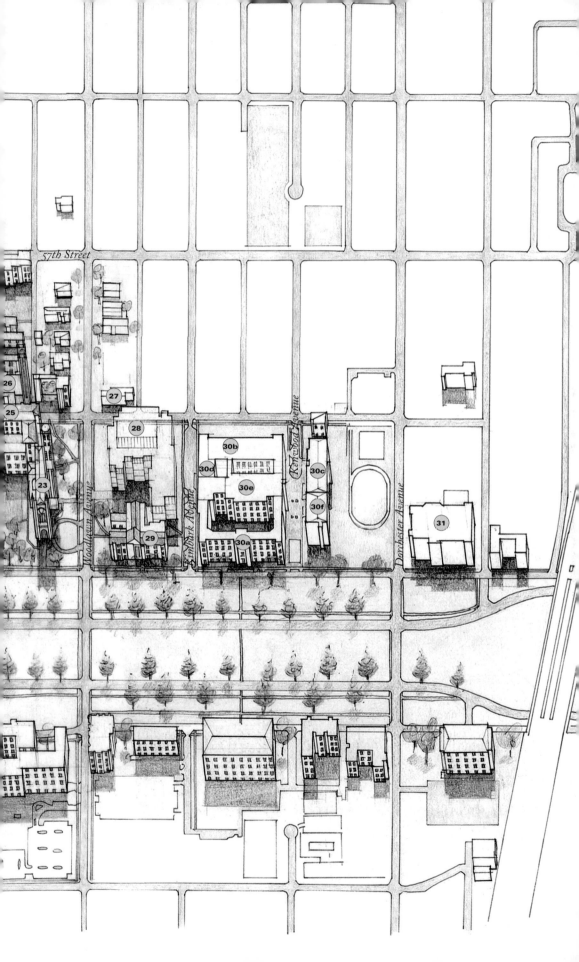

57th Street

Woodlawn Avenue

Kimbark Avenue

Kenwood Avenue

Dorchester Avenue

26

25

23

27

28

29

30a

30b

30d

30e

30c

30f

31

The Enterprising University

The university's cohesive architectural plan was a credit to Henry Ives Cobb, but the fact that the university thrived and evolved with such vigor was due largely to its first president, William Rainey Harper, whose ideas for the university took off from the first and developed a life of their own when he was gone. As we tour what is known as the East Campus, built largely but not entirely in the 1920s when the Main Quadrangles were almost filled, we witness the lasting legacy of both the president and his architect. Cobb had moved on in 1901; Harper died prematurely in 1906. While neither left specific instructions to successors, the university's plan and its architecture were clear and strong, and in the decades that followed, different administrators and architects operated much as Harper and Cobb might have wished. Harper's elaborate program for the university outlined vast synergies between research, publishing, life-long learning extensions, and ties with the worldly professions. Synoptically, his university would be a collection of lively academic enterprises, run by powerful personalities and geared to having an impact on society at large. The East Campus bears witness to this plan's success.

One of many powerful fiefdoms was James Henry Breasted's Oriental Institute. Hired by Harper as a young man, Breasted held the then unconventional belief that civilization did not begin in Ancient Greece but in the Near East. As he popularized this view, he was also able to establish the Oriental Institute as one of the field's leading research centers. In a similar vein, East Campus is also the site of the Laboratory Schools, founded during Harper's administration by John Dewey, the philosopher and specialist in education. By the turn of the century, Dewey and his colleagues had created what was praised by a speaker at the National Council of Education as the most avidly followed school in the country.

Other intellectual enterprises took root, many of them semi-independent but tied to the university in various ways, including architectural style. Ida Noyes Hall, the women's commons, went up in 1916, designed with a mission that is identified with, though not named for, Marion Talbot, the women's dean whose ideas for university women involved powerful individualism and expressive environments for learning. There is International House, based on the gaping need to help foreign students assimilate. And Rockefeller Chapel in particular assumed a unique role from the time it was completed in 1928, providing an ecumenical and eventually political influence to the university community at large.

These enterprises exhibited an independence and strength that drew from Harper's original idea. Their collective architectural character exhibited strength as well, as the Gothic changed and evolved but largely followed the idea of Cobb's revived Gothic, which was vital, versatile, and in many ways modern.

It is best to begin this walk with the massive and extraordinary Rockefeller Chapel, a grand Gothic monument that was at the same time remarkably modern when it was built. Bertram Grosvenor Goodhue began his career in the late 1880s as an unreconstructed traditionalist in the office of James Renwick, designer of St. Patrick's Cathedral in New York. For most of the period of his partnership with the ultra-conservative Ralph Adams Cram (which began in 1890), his designs continued to intentionally evoke Old England. But by the 1920s, Goodhue broke with Cram and embraced a measure of modernity, employing in his designs the flat planes and simplified geometry that would characterize the twentieth century. Rockefeller Chapel is one of Goodhue's best examples of how harmonious the blend of medieval and modern can be.

The chapel was part of John D. Rockefeller's "final gift" to the university in 1910. It should be a "central and dominant feature" on campus, he instructed, and leave no question but that the university was "penetrated by the spirit of religion, all its departments are inspired by the religious feeling, and all its work is dedicated to the highest end." It was without too much debate that the commission went to Goodhue, who was considered the preeminent architect (along with Cram perhaps) of Gothic churches in America. His portfolio included such masterpieces as the chapel at West Point and St. Bartholomew's in New York City. At Chicago, Goodhue did not disappoint, even though the architect did not live to see the work completed. Rockefeller Memorial Chapel (as it was renamed after the donor's death in 1937) is variously cited as the architectural masterpiece of the university, as Goodhue's greatest work, and even, by a hyperbolic Chicago journalist, as one of the most beautiful buildings in the United States. These superlatives are worth mentioning because initially the university was not happy with Goodhue's design schemes.

In the last decade of his career, Goodhue had moved to a style he called "modern Gothic." While his work was influenced by the simplified rules of modern art and architecture, he was equally determined to remain true to the purity of masonry piers, fanned ribs, and "buttresses that actually butt," as the architect liked to say. In fact, his early design proposal was both very grand and seemingly very modern, so much so it made President Burton worry not just about the budget but also about Goodhue's increasing modernity being "too cold and hard and without charm," as he put it in a letter to one of his trustees.

Goodhue was irritated by these criticisms but presented several more possible designs. The one that was chosen placed the tower to the side, a savings over the earlier design with a larger tower above the crossing, but still a structure of size and power. The five bays of the nave are each forty feet square, more than double the standard size in most Gothic

LEFT: *Rockfeller Memorial Chapel, detail*
RIGHT: *"The March of Religion"*

churches. The exterior exhibits flat, unadorned surfaces, but in equal measure the warmth of intricate detail, so much so that the result would certainly have pleased Burton, who also died before the building was completed. Handcrafts are evident in the many carved figures and symbols decorating the chapel inside and out; even the texture of its stone blocks appears hand-hewn, giving the surface a subtle life.

On the front facade, which faces the Midway, deep shadows and heavy piers at the base give way to a shallower and lighter structure as the eye moves upward, a standard Gothic convention. Here it continues dramatically all the way to the roof line where the building's mass dissolves into a complexity of niches, which are occupied by full-size figures and a tableau depicting "The March of Religion." Besides being a design triumph, Goodhue's "March" represents a remarkable ecumenicism with (from left to right) Abraham, Moses, Elijah, Isaiah, Zoroaster, Plato, John the Baptist, Christ (at the peak), Peter, Paul, Athanasius, Augustine, St. Francis, Martin Luther, and finally John Calvin.

The symbolism of these and other ornamental elements were as deeply thought-out as the architectural design—mostly by a committee of faculty and others who determined the messages that they should contain. In the parapet above the front doors, for example, are the shields of many great American universities, including the University of Chicago. Elsewhere are relief sculptures of U.S. presidents Theodore Roosevelt and Woodrow Wilson accompanied by the shields of their alma maters, Harvard and Princeton, respectively. Figures of Dante with the lily of Florence and Milton with the Arms of England are present by one of the side doors. Architect Goodhue is depicted here, too, in a nearly full-size figure in relief, with a model of this chapel in his hand and an image of the chapel at West Point behind his shoulder.

Among the many roles intended for this chapel was serving as a place of music. Its acoustics are duly designed to a high level of performance, with a vaulted ceiling of Guastavino tiles, a then new sound-absorbing

OPPOSITE: *Rockefeller Chapel*

LEFT: *Rockefeller Chapel, carillon*
RIGHT: *Rockefeller Chapel, interior with organ at the right*

material that Goodhue arranged into colorful panels and medallions. An organ by the master organ builder E. M. Skinner was installed, reputed to be one of his most ethereal and nuanced instruments, not to mention one of his largest. And overhead in the tower is one of the world's largest carillons with seventy-two bells that range from twelve pounds to eighteen tons.

The many intricate pieces of the chapel's interior include carved pendants in the organ screen (trumpeting angels) and below the choir gallery at the south end of the nave (reliefs of parables from the gospels), which were carved by Alois Lang of a fabled family of artisans from Oberammergau, Germany. Behind the intricate reredos in the chancel are niches for the ashes of the university's presidents, not all of whom have availed themselves of this privilege.

As an important center of university activity, Rockefeller Chapel has become known for its independence and even political rancor from time to time. It has been committed to interfaith initiatives, and a dean of the chapel some years ago removed all distinctly Christian trappings from the non-architectural decor. Since then, it has become a place where room has been made for Christians, Jews, Muslims, and also "happy agnostics," as a dean once put it. In addition many secular events take place here, such as a great university dinner that was staged on a platform above the pews and organ-accompanied screenings of silent classics like *The Hunchback of Notre Dame*.

24. President's House *Henry Ives Cobb, 1895*

President's House

Even though early budgets were stretched to the limit, the founding trustees were determined to build an on-campus home for the president. The lot was purchased as one of the university's early acquisitions of land beyond the original four-block tract of the Main Quadrangles. To give it a domestic appearance and save construction costs, the house was built of brick instead of limestone. Its massing is much like Cobb's simpler academic buildings, though it lacks the ornate carving around the entrance that was mandatory even on Cobb's most stripped-down limestone buildings. From a distance, the picturesque composition of gables at the roof appears welcoming, but up close, the design turns out to be one of Cobb's most "institutional" ones, in the sense that it is plain and unadorned. In the 1930s, President Hutchins's wife Maude, who was an artist, found the place heavy and dark and encouraged a modernization of the exterior. Unfortunately, one change was the removal of a porch overlooking the Midway, which made its profile even more forbidding than before.

25. Oriental Institute *Mayers, Murray and Phillip, 1931*

Addition *Hammond, Beeby & Babka, 1998*

In the late 1920s there was some thought that all buildings adjacent to Rockefeller Chapel be tied together with a cloister. The idea was never executed, however, perhaps because these buildings represented relatively unrelated centers of authority. The chapel was one, the President's House another. The Oriental Institute, with outposts around the world, also distinguished itself as a true and independent seat of power.

 The building was envisioned, and still serves as, a large museum with an auditorium, classrooms, and offices for scholarly activity. Among the latter are lexigraphical projects, such as the Assyrian and Hittite dictionaries, that have been in progress for decades. Financed by Rockefeller money, the Oriental Institute shows similarities to the chapel— naturally enough, as they were built within three years of one another, designed by the same studio (then called Mayers, Murray and Phillip, successor to Goodhue Associates after Bertram Goodhue's death). The architects certainly intended for the institute to harmonize with if not resemble Goodhue's modern Gothic chapel. But for reasons of fashion

TOP: *Oriental Institute, interior*
BOTTOM: *Oriental Institute, gallery*

LEFT: *Oriental Institute, detail*
RIGHT: *Oriental Institute, entrance*

and a few characteristic design features, this one is commonly tagged
"Art Deco."

The building's simplified Gothic exterior is indeed notable for
planes and masses similar to those of Art Deco or Art Moderne commercial
buildings of the period, such as Chicago's Board of Trade (1930). The tym-
panum over the front door reveals a machine-age sensibility as well,
grafted onto a handcrafted Gothic one: a tableau of icons from the distant
and not-so-distant past, from ancient kings to modern skyscrapers.
Egyptian-like decor was fashionable when the Oriental Institute was built—
due largely to the discovery of King Tut's tomb in 1924—and inspired colorful patterns on the beams overhead, decorative wrought ironwork, and
other ornament that could be described as "Egyptian Art Deco." James
Henry Breasted (see page 72) was not much involved in the architecture of
his research institute, but he did make certain that the gate of Sargon's
palace at Khorsabad, excavated by an Oriental Institute expedition in Syria,
could be installed at the end of a long gallery space; it was lowered into
place before the building was entirely enclosed. Another original artifact of
the galleries was a massive stone sculpture of Tutankamen, a monolith that
requires special supports beneath the gallery floor.

Despite its exotic and modern touches, the Oriental Institute remains
an integrated part of the Gothic revival campus. Lancet windows and trefoil
tracery are obvious adaptations of the Old English–style campus. And its
gables and gray stone, as well as its bays and buttresses show that the Gothic
revival was still regnant in the early 1930s. A recent new wing by Hammond,
Beeby & Babka, used mostly for storage, is essentially a limestone box with
Gothic detail lightly incised in the surface. This addition is relatively unnotice-
able and does little to compromise the timelessness of the structure.

26. Chicago Theological Seminary/Lawson Tower

Herbert Riddle, 1928

The Chicago Theological Seminary moved to Hyde Park ostensibly to join what was evolving as a cluster of seminaries within the orbit of the university. The move was not universally endorsed by those involved, however, since the influence of the university was regarded as suspect to many connected to the old (founded 1855) Congregationalist Seminary. At issue was the university's Divinity School, regarded by many practicing preachers as a "hall of atheists" for its often secular and avowedly scientific approach to the Word of God. Still, the leaders of the seminary (now connected to the United Church of Christ) considered the move a net gain.

As there was no need or desire to identify too closely with the limestone gray of the university, the new seminary buildings were executed in brick. Most prominent among them is the Victor Lawson Tower, named after the late *Chicago Daily News* publisher. Its design was settled after some dispute, as one faction of the seminary directors wanted a spire and others a square tower. Because the latter type was associated with educational institutions, and the former with churches, a compromise was struck with a square tower and lantern atop. The design is reminiscent of the parish church tower of Boston Stump (1520) in Essex County, England. Closer to the ground, a graceful cloister has stones from religious sites around the world embedded in the wall. The chapel's windows are patterned after the stained glass in Chartres Cathedral (mid-1200s) in France.

27. Robie House *Frank Lloyd Wright, 1909*

Robie House was acquired, not built, by the university, and its architecture is utterly contrary to the English Perpendicular style that was enforced for five decades. Yet it is the most famous building on campus and, incidentally, served as a leitmotif for the university's largest-to-date work of twenty-first-century architecture, Rafael Viñoly's Hyde Park Center. Frank Lloyd Wright was normally at odds with but never absent from the rest of the world, and Robie House is a vivid example of his power to affect the environment.

It was built as a residence for bicycle manufacturer Frederick Robie and his wife Lora, a 1900 graduate of the college who wanted to remain in Hyde Park. The oft-told story goes that Robie specified large sunlit spaces, not "absolutely cut up inside" like a typical Queen Anne, as the client later described. Nor did he want "great big stairwells, occupying a lot of valuable space." Robie's need for light, preference for flowing spaces, desire for

OPPOSITE: *Chicago Theological Seminary/Lawson Tower*

privacy but a clear view to the street lined up nicely with Wright's design objectives at the time. The result is a long brick structure with exaggerated eaves and nearly unbroken courses of glass. It remains a classic, perhaps *the* classic, Prairie-style house.

Wright was often effusive, if not always truthful, about the sources of his ideas. He usually stressed that his success was due to his own towering genius, although he frequently expressed admiration for John Ruskin and other English architects associated with the arts and crafts movement. He sometimes even called himself a "Gothic" architect, even though Robie House is one of the most horizontal designs of the era. What Wright clearly shared with the Gothics was a belief that design should be determined by structure and that good architecture was created from the inside out. Robie's asymmetry is another connection with the Gothic, as is its staunch (albeit picturesque) protection from the outside.

Robie House became a lightning rod of the preservation movement in the 1950s after the Chicago Theological Seminary acquired it for a dormitory, then made plans to tear it down for a more capacious structure. "We are in the business to educate ministers, not to support a national shrine," said the seminary's business manager at the time. Wright himself declared that destroying Robie House would be a "special species of vandalism," though "a religious organization has no sense of beauty. You can't expect much from them." The problem was resolved when William Zeckendorf, a New York developer involved in Hyde Park's urban renewal project, bought it for use as an office. It was later donated to the university—much worse for wear by then, for which Wright blamed the seminarians who lived there and "made whoopee, you know." The consensus view is that Wright's engineering skills did not match his innovative designs. Unlike the hard stone of Gothic architecture that gets stronger with age, things fall apart in many Wright houses.

Robie House has served the university in various capacities. In 1966, it was made headquarters of the Adlai Stevenson Institute, a center for the study of international diplomacy and in 1970 was subject to an attack, with broken windows and smashed furniture (there is no record that Wright material was lost), when anti-war demonstrators suspected the institute of involvement in U.S. policy in Vietnam. In 1980 it was occupied by the Alumni Affairs office, which remained there until 1997, when the university joined with the Frank Lloyd Wright Preservation Trust (then the Frank Lloyd Wright Home and Studio Foundation) to engage in fundraising, preservation, and creation of a proper house museum.

Time has treated Robie House well. It needs constant repair but still appears modern, even though it is two full decades older than the ancient-looking Rockefeller Chapel across the street.

TOP: *Robie House, south facade*
BOTTOM: *Robie House, with Hyde Park Center in foreground*

Graduate School of Business, Hyde Park Center

28. Graduate School of Business, Hyde Park Center

Rafael Viñoly, 2004

As this text is written, the Hyde Park Center, built to satisfy the needs of the university's Graduate School of Business, is almost brand-new. Its architect, Rafael Viñoly, emerged as the victor in a competition that included Pei Cobb Freed & Partners of New York, Rafael Moneo of Madrid, and others of equally high stature. Perhaps better than the others, Viñoly's design endeavors to bridge the stylistic gulf between the Prairie style of Robie House directly across the street and the prevailing Gothic on the rest of campus. The result can be judged as a harmonious blend of modern and Gothic architecture.

In fact, the building's so-called Gothic elements are mostly inside. Tubular steel arches support a spectacular cathedral ceiling in the central building element, a six-story glass-enclosed winter garden. An outdoor courtyard provides views of Ida Noyes and the Rockefeller Chapel. But on the exterior, Viñoly genuflects extravagantly to modernism, echoing Wright's Robie House in the center's emphatic horizontal lines and interlocking cubes clad in smooth limestone panels.

Viñoly shows that modern construction technology has made the formal possibilities of architecture—such as the blending of Gothic and Prairie styles, for example—nearly limitless. Large enough to accommodate

Graduate School of Business, Hyde Park Center, interior

the whole school comfortably, the building's infrastructure features built-in telecommunications, wireless networking, and state-of-the-art audio-visual systems in its twelve classrooms.

29. Ida Noyes Hall   *Shepley, Rutan and Coolidge, 1916*

Before Ida Noyes Hall, named for the deceased wife of a Chicago inventor and businessman, was dedicated in 1916, the frugal President Judson intimated that it was too costly, too luxurious, simply too much for a university that had been overspending (he believed) since its founding. But the building, originally a women's commons and gymnasium, had an important objective. As Marion Talbot, Dean of Women and tireless champion of the university women, argued, Noyes Hall would edify the student and encourage "forms of social expression which will make her academic training more effective as she mingles among people."

There are definite notes of domesticity in the design. Features of a Tudor manor house are emphasized with half-timber work, lacily carved windows, and rows of dormer-like gables overhead. A cloister on the west side provides an intimate way to enter from campus, while a stately front facing the Midway made clear that the building counted among the important ones of the growing university. The interior design remains lavish, with

LEFT: *Ida Noyes Hall, mural*
RIGHT: *Ida Noyes Hall*

wood paneling, intricately plastered ceilings, fine paving tiles, ornate stair rails, and didactic pre-Raphaelite murals in the third-floor theater. It is actually a curious mix of styles—mostly Gothic, of course, but with touches of classical and infusions of arts and crafts. Many such touches remain even as the building has been transformed from a place of refined domesticity to a co-ed clubhouse, including a 450-seat movie theater, which more than any other change has made Ida Noyes a true center of student activity.

30. Laboratory Schools

Emmons Blaine Hall *James Gamble Rogers, 1903*

Henry Holmes Belfield Hall *James Gamble Rogers, 1904*

Bernard E. Sunny Gym *Armstrong, Furst and Tilton, 1929*

Charles Judd Hall *Armstrong, Furst and Tilton, 1931*

University High School *Perkins and Will, 1960*

Kovler Gym *Nagle, Hartray, Danker, Kagan, McKay, 2000*

The University Laboratory Schools were another unique enterprise inspired by President Harper's eagerness to establish "affiliated institutions" in the university's wide-ranging academic environment. Once integral parts of the university's education department, "Lab" remains one of the city's most desirable private schools. The Laboratory Schools were founded at different times and under different circumstances, but there is nothing in the architecture to suggest that they are not full-fledged parts of the University of Chicago. Here, the original buildings, Blaine Hall and Belfield Hall, were designed by James Gamble Rogers, a beaux-arts architect from the East previously known for neoclassical design. Rogers took to the Gothic very well, going on to design other major academic buildings in the style such as Deering Library at Northwestern (1933) and Harkness Tower at Yale (1922).

The history of the Laboratory Schools began with the "pragmatist" philosopher John Dewey, whom Harper had brought to Chicago in 1894 to head the university's Department of Philosophy, Psychology, and Pedagogy. Dewey's modern approach to childhood education was based on creating a sense of community and spontaneous discovery in classrooms, and the "Dewey School," as it was called at the time, enjoyed early success in making believers of many parents. In 1901 Harper sought to expand this enterprise and convinced the Chicago Institute, a new elementary school and teacher college founded by Francis Wayland Parker, to merge with Dewey. Equally progressive, the institute was lavishly funded by benefactor Mrs. Emmons Blaine, a member of the Cyrus McCormick family. Blaine had already chosen Rogers as architect when the decision was made to build in Hyde Park. Despite some initial rivalry between Dewey's and Parker's schools, they moved together into Blaine Hall in 1903.

A year later, Harper's capacity to lure affiliates brought to campus a pair of high schools, the South Side Academy and the Chicago Manual

Laboratory Schools, with Belfield Hall, Judd Hall, and Blaine Hall from left to right

Blaine Hall

Training School to create what was later called the University High School. Again there was initial rivalry between the schools, but Belfield Hall's strong architecture helped create a new identity. Early success of University High's football team was also helpful in building school spirit.

Rogers came to these commissions with a strictly beaux-arts sensibility, visible especially in the rigorous symmetry of Blaine Hall's floor plan. Gothic randomness was not in his mind when he designed Blaine, rather the architect was interested in wide halls and interior traffic flow. And because the school was also a memorial to Mrs. Blaine's husband, Rogers was intent on designing a building "as monumental as possible without departing from its own simple character." The result is a design that employs elements of the Cobbian vocabulary—limestone, turrets, and finials—that blend the buildings easily into the general fabric of the university. But the style appears more fitting to a French Renaissance chateau than a proper Gothic castle.

In 1931 the Rogers buildings were connected by Charles Judd Hall, designed by Armstrong, Furst and Tilton, a Chicago firm whose credits are largely in churches, notably the Episcopal seminary in Evanston. Judd Hall fits in with Rogers's previous buildings with random ease. The same firm designed Sunny Gym in 1929, a solid Gothic revival design, modernized in its time with de-elaborated details such as simple decoration in windows and a parapet so shallow that it is almost imperceptible.

Connected to Sunny on the south is the recent Kovler Gym, a rare charming exercise in postmodernism. Kovler's design is even more

University High

restrained than that of Sunny next door. Its most striking element is inside: a narrow atrium between the new and old buildings, which uses the trac-eried windows that were once on Sunny's exterior as a dramatic interior element. Around Kovler are carved stone panels by Walter Arnold, one of the few artisans still carving architectural stone. His subjects include mod-ern sports, and their effect is substantially pre-modern.

In 1960 a modernist addition to house University High was inserted within the ample courtyard between Blaine and Belfield halls. Designed by Perkins and Will, its aluminum and glass exterior could hardly be more dif-ferent from the Gothic of the original building. An arcade of pointed alu-minum arches refers to the gables of Blaine and Belfield and its largely open interior corresponds to the largely open space of the old buildings. Mercifully, perhaps, the clash of this addition with the rest of the campus is safely hidden from view.

31. International House *Holabird and Root, 1931*

When established, International House was part-independent agency and part-university affiliate. The architectural influences of its building are like-wise mixed, with elements of university Gothic, Art Deco skyscraper, and even a touch of colonial-revival. The history of the institution began in 1910 when a YMCA worker in New York worried that foreign students at

International House

Columbia University needed improved social outlets. Within a few years, John D. Rockefeller, Jr. funded International House to promote understanding among students, first at Columbia and later at several other institutions, including the University of Chicago.

　　The university, which was responsible for siting the structure and getting it built, bought an old hotel at Blackstone and razed it to make room. The commission to design the five-hundred-room dormitory project went to Holabird and Root, in part because the firm had extensive experience in large commercial projects. University architect Emery Jackson was also involved, specifying that International House "shouldn't be a skyscraper for I do not think a tall building would harmonize with the prevailing architecture of the university community." Still, its size would necessitate architecture unlike anything else on campus, and for this reason early schemes might have appeared too commercial in nature. When a Rockefeller executive reviewed them, he suggested "a greater degree of harmonization between the Gothic aspect and the modern aspects."

When the building finally opened in 1931, it was described as "of Indiana limestone and of Gothic architecture to harmonize with the university building." In retrospect, of course, it is a departure in many ways. Unlike most other buildings on campus, it is of reinforced concrete, not steel frame, and its size and setbacks resemble more a streamlined high-rise from the 1920s than the English Perpendicular of the quadrangles. Curiously, the interior of International House was designed with an antique feel though not a Gothic one. Perhaps to promote the idea of Americanism, common rooms were originally colonial in style with Chippendale, Sheraton, and Duncan Phyfe pieces echoing "an 18th century drawing room," as described by the *University Record*.

International House is not a stirring landmark of architecture, but it does demonstrate another adaptation of the university's architectural template. Simultaneously, it shows how much the Art Deco commercial style was influenced by the Gothic revival. One need only recall the Chicago Tribune Tower competition where several of the entries, including the winning scheme, combined a vertical modern structure with Gothic-like ornament. International House demonstrates the converse: that a resolutely Gothic campus could also adopt the massing and abstract modern ornament of the Jazz Age.

International House, entrance detail

South of the Midway

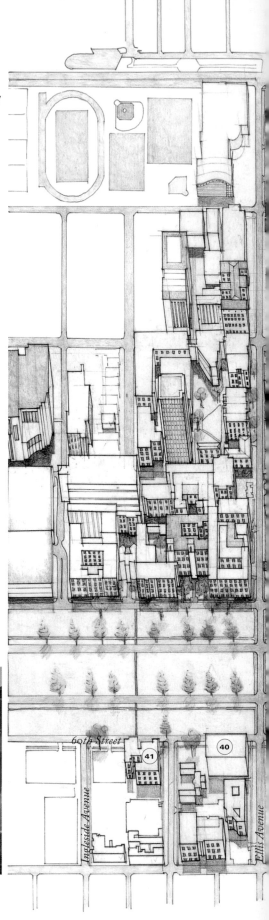

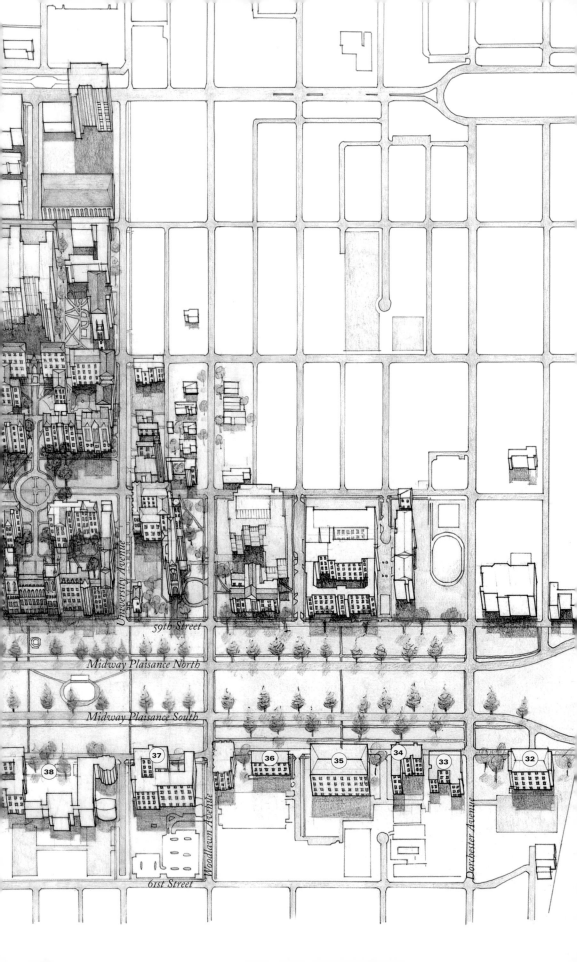

University Avenue

59th Street

Midway Plaisance North

Midway Plaisance South

Woodlawn Avenue

Dorchester Avenue

61st Street

38

37

36

35

34

33

32

Modernism on the Midway

Moving south of the Midway, we will witness architecture that is largely distant from the rest of the campus in terms of space, time, and style. Since 1907 the university has owned and controlled most of both sides of the Midway, but the land along Sixtieth Street remained largely unused for decades thereafter. The first developments came in the 1930s when two buildings in the traditional campus style were built there, richly appointed, though later dismissed as the "last gasp" of Chicago Gothic, suggesting that the campus had grown tired of the old boilerplate.

It was mostly after World War II, when American architecture was in the thrall of postwar modernism, that the university developed the Midway's south edge. Unfortunately, true modern architecture, just a few decades old at the time, was still a hit-or-miss proposition. More bluntly, at least half the modern buildings south of the Midway have not stood the test of time.

Admittedly, the Midway is not an easy place to site individual buildings; it is a vast tract where architecture easily gets lost. In fact, it was laid out with little thought of the buildings that would surround it (which makes the university's "facade" along the north edge all the more impressive). Its history goes back to the 1860s when the nation's leading landscape architects, Frederick Law Olmsted and Calvert Vaux, designed a system of parks for Chicago's South Side. To achieve variety, Olmsted and Vaux created two separate parks, Jackson and Washington, one on the shore, the other on the prairie, and connected them with this mile-long green belt they called Midway Plaisance.

While Olmsted's ideas about landscape ranged from severe order to wild naturalism, the Midway itself was designed as a simple stretch of land with trees and winding carriage ways. In 1893 it was transformed into a portion of the site dedicated to the World's Columbian Exposition—remembered today for the world's first Ferris wheel, the era's most lascivious belly dancer ("Little Egypt"), and the introduction of the word "midway" into the American lexicon.

After the fair, an elderly Olmsted suggested a canal to run the length of the Midway with monumental bridges crossing over it. The water concept more or less faded when Olmsted died in 1903, though the great neo-classical sculptor Lorado Taft revived this idea in 1910 and added a plan to line both sides of the canal with sculpture. Taft, with a little help from the university, where he was a part-time teacher, created *The Fountain of Time*, a massive sculptural tableau at the west end of the Midway, but his plan got no further.

The university's actual expansion across the Midway began in 1931, when the Burton-Judson dormitory complex was built on Sixtieth Street.

Depression and World War II slowed the southward migration of campus, but it would resume inevitably after the war. That was when the Midway figured prominently into a new campus plan by Eero Saarinen, commissioned as the university's consulting architect in 1954. Saarinen was one of America's leading modernists at the time, noted for romantic expression in the otherwise stripped-down efficiency of modernism. Saarinen's Cranbrook School (designed with his father Eliel) and General Motors Technology Center demonstrated that campuses could be modern and have artistic flourish as well.

At the University of Chicago, Saarinen's general objective was to open long landscaped vistas on campus, the most important of which would be the Midway. To that effect he devised a scheme to redirect Midway vehicular traffic south and to create what would probably have been the world's largest academic quadrangle. As he rendered the idea, the architect also drew a new building—it was never specified for what—to straddle the Midway at Dorchester, proposing an enclosed area and new geographical center of the university.

Most of Saarinen's plans were not executed, partly because he died prematurely in 1961. What Saarinen did accomplish was to place the Law School south of the Midway with the Laird Bell Quadrangle, a stellar modern complex that referred to the Gothic but did so without submitting to the traditional Bedford limestone monopoly. Today, we appreciate the Law School because it is both of its own time and harmonizes with the Gothic revival, which it abuts on the east end of Burton-Judson.

32. University Press Building   *Booth Hansen Associates, 2001*

University Press Building

The Gothic-style profile and color of this building hark to the early 1900s; its postmodern revival of a (Gothic) revival style is pure 1990s. Laurence Booth was chosen as architect of this much needed building, which provided 90,000 square feet to help consolidate the vast operation of the University of Chicago Press, the nation's largest university publishing house.

Booth enjoys a wide reputation in Chicago as an architect who brings architectural flair to large projects. Early in his career he was distinguished for his rebellion against the Miesian canon (of less-is-more/glass-and-steel) and embraced the postmodern notion that elements of architectural history could be incorporated in useful and comfortable contemporary architecture. In the Press Building,

Orthogenic School

the cast-concrete resembles limestone and the molded Gothic arches recall the old campus template. In the end, however, the design quickly became a thing of the past. This inoffensive building is likely to be the final attempt to produce so figuratively an echo of old buildings in the new ones of the future.

33. Orthogenic School *Coolidge and Hodgdon, 1927, I. W. Colburn, 1965*

The Orthogenic School was affiliated with the university in the 1940s when it took occupancy of two structures that had been outside but adjacent to the southeastern edge of campus: the Georgian-style church and parish house of St. Paul's Universalist Church. (The church probably chose this site because university trustee Charles Hutchinson was a Universalist; Coolidge and Hodgson were his favorite architects.) The Orthogenic School's mission is to house and teach emotionally disturbed children, and a 1965 addition that connects the two older buildings aptly suggests that the complex no longer houses a church. Designed by Chicago architect I. W. "Ike" Colburn, it presents a stark modern facade with touches of a severe Tuscan fortress.

Protection from the outside certainly lined up with the theories of the school's most famous director, Dr. Bruno Bettelheim, a Nazi concentration camp survivor who tried to create a tiny community in his school where students might thrive. At the dedication of the Coburn addition, Bettelheim said, "It is their alienation from the world at large, combined

Chapin Hall Center for Children

SOUTH OF THE MIDWAY

97

with the anomie and anonymity of our big cities, which results in so many of our adolescents feeling that they are of no account." Bettelheim indicated that he drew his theories partly from the work of John Dewey (see Laboratory Schools), and partly from his countryman Sigmund Freud. Just as Bettelheim's school represents a mix of American and European influences, its architecture is a similar not-too-harmonious blend. The colonial-revival parish house and church express the welcome and openness of a sleepy New England village, while the medieval-modern addition seems bent on keeping the world out. In front of the 1965 addition is a loggia with a ceramic mural by Spaniard Jordi Bonet featuring abstract human figures over what appears to be a scorched landscape streaked with rich and beautiful colors.

34. Chapin Hall Center for Children (formerly the Merriam Center) *Zantzinger and Borie, 1938*

Renovation *VOA Associates, 1996*

The Merriam Center was constructed on land on the Midway as a group headquarters for various national government associations, or the "Public Administration Clearing House." With funding from the Rockefeller Foundation, the building went up in 1938 in the Gothic revival style that emphasized its affiliation with the university. It was named in honor of Charles Merriam, a professor and political activist who twice ran for

Chapin Hall, detail

Chicago mayor on a reformist "good government" platform. Merriam believed ties between his political science department and national groups (such as the American Society of Planning Officials and National Association of Assessing Officers) would be mutually beneficial.

Designed by Philadelphia architects Zantzinger and Borie (who by this time had lost the firm's true Gothicist partner Medary), the center has been referred to as "amiably Gothic." Like the Burton-Judson dormitory, its variegated limestone blocks and exterior carving reflect a richness that was not widespread in 1938. Inside, quarter-sawn oak paneling graces the conference room, and brushed aluminum rails and elevators typify the high Art Deco tastes of the time. The Merriam Center also had the university's first building-wide air-conditioning system. Perhaps more interesting than its architecture, however, were public reactions to the building. Initially designated only by its address, 1313 East Sixtieth, it was accused by some of a numerological connection with witchcraft. More revealing of the postwar times, McCarthy-wing conservatives attacked the associations headquartered there for "collectivized Metropolitan Government."

When the local and state government associations moved out in the 1990s, the building was occupied by the Chapin Hall Center for Children, a venerable organization with roots as a nineteenth-century orphanage, now a university-affiliated research center. A retrofit, which saved and highlighted rich wood trim and aluminum fixtures inside, was executed in 1996. The director of Chapin Hall has noted that the fine interiors and L-shaped floor plan of the original building remain key in making it a "public commons, a site for the exchange of ideas."

35. New Graduate Residence (formerly the Center of Continuing Education) *Edward Durrell Stone, 1962*

Experiments with new materials and new forms were rampant in postwar architecture—not all successful or even well-thought out. And since these were prosperous times, promiscuous and unfortunate construction went on everywhere in America. The university did not escape; Sixtieth Street, in particular, is now lined with a collection of buildings that represent a "museum" of strange days in American architecture.

LEFT: *New Graduate Residence*
RIGHT: *New Graduate Residence, concrete pillars*

Stone's Center of Continuing Education is almost too easy a target. Stone, who had been co-designer of the Museum of Modern Art in New York in 1938 and who died in 1972, was regarded as a master modernist, though his shortcomings were increasingly recognized as his career progressed. His early home designs are well-proportioned with constructivist restraint. But the architect later grew bored with plain geometric precision and devised decorative techniques to embellish (and he believed soften) the surfaces of his buildings. Today, his name is often mentioned in connection with a preservation controversy over his 2 Columbus Circle in New York, built in the 1960s, which uses semi-Moorish designs that even those who are trying to save the building find unappealing.

On Chicago's Midway, Stone built a broadly horizontal building with seventy-two thin concrete pillars around it—a modernist take on Greek revival perhaps, except that the pillars and the walls are incised with an abstract design that may be Moorish or perhaps a vague reference to the Gothic. It seems the massive open spaces of the Midway inspired Stone to move away from anything Perpendicular, and sadly away from a design that would resonate in its place or even its time. In addition, the overall design and construction have aged badly; the dated ornament decorates a structure that is discolored and decayed. Today the building serves as a residence for graduate students.

TOP: *Charles Stewart Mott Building*
BOTTOM: *1155 East Sixtieth Street*

Schmidt, Garden and Erikson, 1959

The Mott Building's architectural virtues are rarely discussed, but there is something curious in the way the broad glass curtain wall is broken into rhythmic sections like a Mondrian puzzle. This could be regarded as a variation on the modernist effort to find beauty in industrial materials. While the great modernists—Mies van der Rohe is the most vivid example—used glass and steel boldly, the architects of this building were less confident. They designed a facade of considerable size but broke it up into smaller, less conspicuous components. Schmidt, Garden and Erikson also integrated limestone as a building material, a careful if ineffectual reference to the campus's past. "The flanking walls of stone are large enough so that an effect of solidity balances the fragility of the glass," wrote a charitable critic in the *Tribune* in 1963.

Mott was built as an industrial relations center to investigate the areas of mutual interest to business and the social sciences. Today it is used for administrative offices of the university, and has lately housed the printing department.

37. 1155 East Sixtieth Street *Holabird and Root, 1954*

This building is pure 1950s, and behind its plainness is some charm. Its massing of interlocking limestone cubes is curious and more thoughtful than other modernist jumbles nearby. The graceful randomness of its massing could even be said to reflect the heterogeneity of tenants for whom the building was designed. It was originally not a university building, but the headquarters of the American Bar Association, which brought with it a variety of other organizations, such as the National Legal Aid and Defender Association and the National Association of Women Lawyers.

The building was placed on university property to encourage the idea that these organizations' practical work could benefit from the legal scholarship at the Law School next door, and vice versa. President Lawrence Kimpton noted in a dedicatory speech for this building that the work of the Bar Center should seek to understand the intersections between law and other academic disciplines, citing atomic energy, discovered just a few blocks away and just a few years before, as an example. Today, the building is occupied primarily by the Harris Graduate School of Public Policy and the National Opinion Research Center.

38. Laird Bell Law Quadrangle *Eero Saarinen, 1959*

From a distance, one might regard the Laird Bell Law Quadrangle as dated, a relic from the 1950s or 1960s. But that is mostly because a generation of imitators that followed Eero Saarinen gave cold war modernism a bad name with bland, faceless designs. Saarinen was in fact one of the few who could sculpt striking architectural form from modern materials. The D'Angelo Law Library, the Law School's most prominent element, does feature some standard-issue modern images such as the serrated glass roofline and a great concrete pool in front. Yet the closer you look at it, the more the building pleases the eye—it is modern and abstract, to be sure, but also in curious sympathy with the old-campus style of Burton-Judson right next door.

Saarinen's pedigree as well as his protean skill as a designer has made him an enormous name in American architecture. He was the son of Eliel Saarinen, whose second place–winning design in the Chicago Tribune competition remains one of the most influential unbuilt skyscrapers ever. That scheme used buttresses and setbacks in a simple, soaring profile, a thoroughly modern skyscraper in essentially Gothic garb, or vice versa.

For his part, Eero was constantly searching for new approaches, in terms of building technology and innovative form, but with a classic touch for the ages. In the Law School, he used reflective, high-performance glass panels (upgraded since original construction) that were then evolving, due in no small part to the automotive industry. Before Chicago, Saarinen fashioned dramatic glass curtain walls for the General Motors Research Center in Michigan.

Saarinen was hardly a gothicist devoted to handcrafts. If anything, he took machine-made materials to an extreme that made the industrial ethic of the Bauhaus architects seem like mere tinkering. Yet the architect believed that modernists at large had failed dismally in achieving harmony with the past, particularly on college campuses. "The primary characteristic of this period seems to be building buildings—buildings thought of as entities in themselves," he wrote in an *Architectural Record* article that focused on his planning work at the university. "Very little has been produced recently in the form of over-all campus building concepts." In fact, Saarinen did not solve the problem in his master plan for the university; he died in 1961, perhaps before he had a fair chance.

But in this largest of the buildings that he designed himself on this campus, Saarinen met his own elusive standard. "By stressing a small, broken scale, a lively silhouette, and especially verticality in the library design, we intend to make it a good neighbor with the neo-Gothic dormitories," Saarinen described his approach. What is remarkable about the Law School is that it responds both to the horizontal cues of its site as well as the vertical ones. The Midway demanded that the Law School complex fill its site,

TOP: *D'Angelo Law Library with sculpture by Antoine Pevsner*
BOTTOM: *D'Angelo Law Library, interior*

LEFT: *Burton-Judson Courts*
RIGHT: *Burton-Judson Courts, lounge*

so as not to be visually swallowed by the parkway. At the same time, the design of the library echoes the perpendicular towers that characterize the Gothic, making the admittedly stark contrast between the new and the old visually interesting.

The library can best be analyzed as a piece of sculpture. The triangular sections give the facade a cool vitality, emphasized by the Dan Kiley–designed poolscape and "constructivist" sculpture by Antoine Pevsner. At the same time, the repose of the design renders a sense of permanence that eludes much other modern architecture.

Also remarkable in the near half-century history of the complex is how Saarinen's studied asymmetricality enabled a 1987 addition to the glass centerpiece without upsetting the picturesque composition of the building or the quadrangle. Professors praise it for its functionality; when new it was unique in its organization of professors' offices around its perimeter, assuring maximum contact between students and faculty.

39. Burton-Judson Courts *Zantzinger, Borie and Medary, 1931*

The re-emphasis of undergraduate life at the university was one of the early achievements of President Robert Maynard Hutchins, who was appointed in 1929. Hutchins instituted a new core curriculum and emphasized teaching from original sources such as Plato and Livy. But even before Hutchins arrived, there were plans to invigorate the college experience by building Burton-Judson around two courtyards and with the most updated lodging and dining facilities possible. Previously, only a small minority of undergraduates lived in residence halls—most lived off-campus and in fraternities. This was a shortcoming that prompted President Burton (Hutchins's predecessor) to fund and build these "College Residence Halls for Men" to facilitate "a constant and healthful interchange of thought and development," as he stated.

OPPOSITE: *Burton-Judson Courts*

The seriousness of the university's intent to design the best possible quarters for undergraduates prompted a committee to travel east to see what other schools had built. The Philadelphia firm of Zantzinger, Borie and Medary had recently completed distinguished "medieval" work, as it was then called, at Yale and Princeton, which impressed these emissaries enough to commission the architects for two buildings. The firm's Gothic renditions at Chicago—Merriam Hall in addition to Burton-Judson—were successful, if not sublime, despite these architects' clear preference for beaux-art neoclassicism. Here a refined Gothic profile of towers and pitched roofs is impressive even from a distance, despite being somewhat dwarfed by the Midway's overall dimensions. Inside, the detailing of two courtyards and dining halls with great timbered beams are striking.

While there was some carping on campus that these dorms should be in a more modern style, the university held fast at this time against mere fashion. "Modern criticism has been too insistently demanding that all our architecture should "express the Machine Age," wrote Hugh Morrison, an art instructor, in the *University of Chicago Magazine*. "This may produce good buildings but it may also result in ugly packing-box tenements. Fine architecture is too varied and elusive a thing to be judged by any such narrow formula." Many buildings that came later would validate this warning from Morrison, who was also the biographer of modernist prophet Louis Sullivan.

The gardens surrounding Burton-Judson were planned by the landscape designer Beatrix Farrand, and playing fields extended from the back of the buildings to Sixty-first Street. The greensward was laid out for baseball and football, and the layout also included tennis courts. There was even "additional space for the introduction of such novel sports as 'bowling on the green,'" as described in a brochure when the doors were opened.

40. School of Social Service Administration
Ludwig Mies van der Rohe, 1963

Like many other glass-and-steel boxes by Mies van der Rohe, this one has a simplicity that becomes more intense, even spiritual, the more you experience it. Mies possessed a zen-like belief in the integrity and beauty of unadorned industrial materials. Thus he makes no attempt to hide the basic construction of glass and steel nor to apply historical references in his designs. His inimitable skill lay in creating sublime compositions from the simplest construction. The geometry of the frame, the transparency of the glass, the tactile nature of the brick walls inside all call attention to themselves individually and contribute indispensably to a space that is both agreeable and amazing.

The Social Service Administration building is not too different from other examples of Mies's universal space, where the divisions within a

School of Social Service Administration

building are only suggested (sometimes by half-walls, other times by glass) just as the boundaries between interior and exterior are dissolved. Inside, one enjoys a kind of dual sensation—the vastness of infinite space outside and a certain intimacy and warmth within. This is postwar modernism at its best. Crown Hall at IIT and Farnsworth House in Plano, Illinois are two other Chicago-area examples by Mies where this very same effect is striking.

In retrospect, Mies was a risky if not downright peculiar choice for a university that prided itself on its English Perpendicular. The commission came about in all likelihood because Mrs. Herbert Greenwald was a member of the School of Social Service's visiting committee (the equivalent of the school's outside directors), and her husband was the visionary real estate developer who commissioned Mies to build 860-880 North Lake Shore Drive, the apartment towers that made Mies famous and steel-and-glass modernism ubiquitous in cities everywhere.

Unlike the rest of the university, which is largely cloistered, Mies's building opens generously to the outside, with split-level mezzanines on either side of the building containing classrooms with glass walls. The sense of free space is so intense, some teachers say, that the classrooms appear to be floating in space a few feet above the Midway outside.

It is certainly an eccentric building, which has its share of problems. The roof tends to leak. And to get from the mezzanine on one side to the mezzanine on the other, occupants have to walk down and then up—or take the elevators that the architect prohibited but which were later installed to comply with disability regulations. But even as offices and classrooms at the school grow crowded, few people begrudge the great glassed-in central

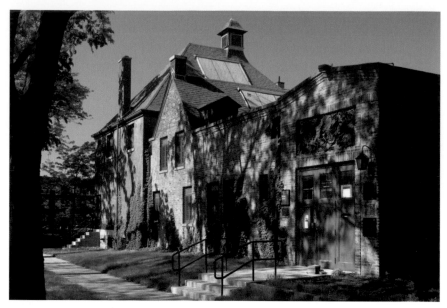

Midway Studios

space where even minor receptions can be dramatic, and a student's bag lunch can be consumed sitting on a Barcelona chair with an unbroken view of the university beyond.

41. Midway Studios *Various architects and builders including Pond and Pond, 1909; and Loebel, Schlossman, Bennett and Dart, 1972*

The worn and weary Midway Studios of the university's art department look almost nothing like the surrounding neo-Gothic buildings. The complex is mostly undistinguished masonry, and the only building with identifiable "architecture" is the 1888 Queen Anne residence on the corner of Ingleside and Sixtieth streets. The studios, cobbled together with brick and concrete buildings, were originally used as a workspace for Lorado Taft, one of the nation's most distinguished sculptors at the turn of the twentieth century.

The complex is an unlikely National Historic Landmark, but it was so designated as a tribute to Taft's stature, not its patchwork architecture. Yet, the place leaves you with the sensation that nothing expresses the Gothic spirit more authentically than these disparate buildings clustered together in an unexpectedly picturesque whole. The Midway Studios demonstrate what Ruskin and his hordes of followers declared: that the most romantic buildings are those that are handcrafted and idiosyncratic. The gentle effects of age and several Tudor gables highlight the effect, per-haps, but true Gothicness of the studios lies in the fact that they were assembled by many hands and many hearts.

Fountain of Time *by Lorado Taft*

The history of the studios goes back to 1906 when Taft left his quarters in the now-venerable Fine Arts Building downtown for space near the Midway. The university provided him with a vacant brick barn on Ellis Avenue about a block from where he and his team of protégées produced the master's many commissioned works in the years that followed. These included the *Fountain of Time*, now at the Midway's west end, along with casts and designs for the unexecuted works that Taft would have placed all around the parkway.

As Taft's work and the number of his followers increased, he built additions onto his studio, and as many as a dozen structures with workrooms, classrooms, and dormitories went up around the original brick barn, including one designed by the esteemed Prairie School office of Pond and Pond. Taft always said that he built the studios "like a chambered nautilus, cell by cell," a high exercise in organic architecture.

Around 1929 the university needed the land on Ellis Avenue and offered Taft and his students the use of land a block west, behind the Queen Anne building that became the master's residence. The barn was moved relatively intact, and other buildings were either moved—perhaps part of the Pond and Pond though this is not certain—or recreated from spare parts of others.

So Midway Studios evolved anew. Most photographed was (and is) the Court Gallery in a central space with a high-gabled ceiling and skylights, used as an exhibition space for Taft's plaster casts of classical sculpture such as *Caesar Augustus* and *La Pieta*. A later exhibit in the gallery featured salvaged ornament that sculptor Alphonso Ianelli produced for Midway Gardens, the Frank Lloyd Wright–designed beer garden built in 1914 a few yards away at Sixtieth Street and Cottage Grove (razed in 1929).

In 1940, four years after Taft's death, the studios reverted back to the university, which today uses them to house studio art classes. Additions continued, including a 1965 studio space with industrial skylights by the Chicago architect Edward Dart. A ceramic lintel by artist Ruth Duckworth, who taught here in the 1960s, gives a barn door on the east side the presence of a semi-stately entrance. Inside is a makeshift courtyard with a large bronze sculpture by Taft and a marble head of Beethoven by an early student. They appear placed here casually, more by fate than intention, and suggest an epigram that remains on the Fine Arts Building, which Taft abandoned before coming here: "Time passes. Only art endures."

FOLLOWING SPREAD: *The Midway with sculpture of Carolus Linneaus by Johan Dyfverman*

The Medical Center

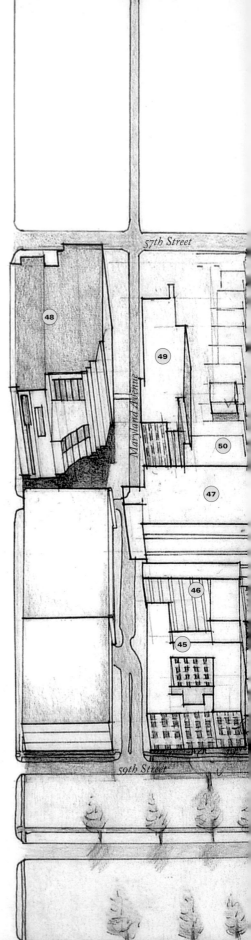

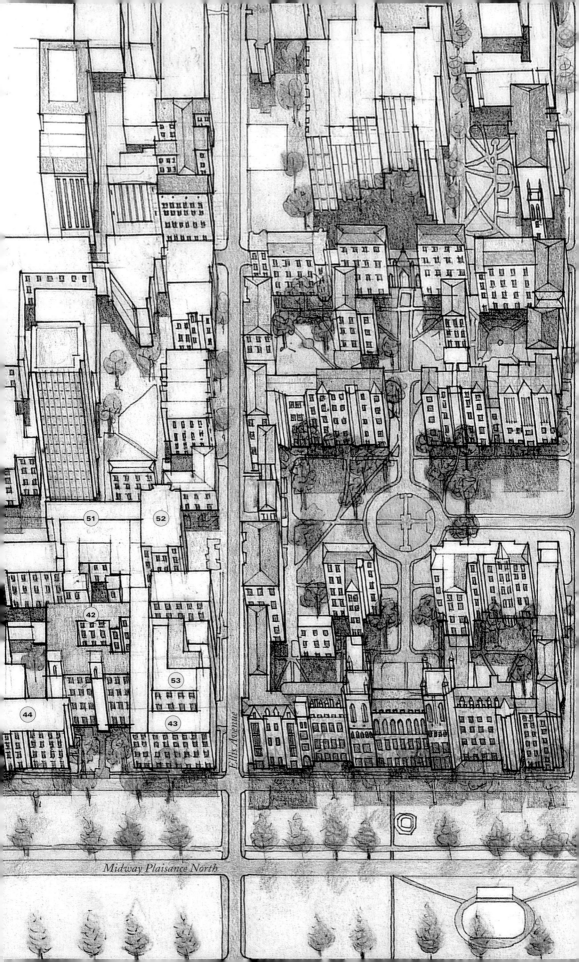

51

52

42

44

53

43

Ellis Avenue

Midway Plaisance North

Center of Research and Healing

Viewing the medical center from the Midway, one could take it for a harmonious extension of the campus. Its facades exhibit the same stolid Gothic as the original quadrangles—the same limestone, the same fine carving, the same general scale. Beneath the surface, or even around the corner, however, substantial differences are visible. The hospital's more recent architecture, for example, ignores the old stone completely. And from the north and the west, the seamlessness gives way to a variety of modern styles.

The history of medicine at the university goes back to 1898 when President Harper affiliated with Rush Medical School on the West Side of Chicago. It was a useful relationship; while many medical schools at the time were for-profit diploma mills and without standards, Rush was held in high regard. Funded in 1844, it had since its beginnings concentrated on conscientious clinical training in several Chicago hospitals and turned out many of the city's most esteemed physicians. Still, the program was somewhat unsatisfactory, primarily because it displeased John D. Rockefeller, whose millions were financing the university. Rockefeller did not believe that Rush's emphasis on clinical training was appropriate for a university that was at its heart a research institution and threatened to walk away from Chicago altogether. Happily, Rockefeller soon relented, and medical students would spend two years in the hospitals associated with Rush after learning basic science in Hyde Park. It was inevitable, however, that the university would eventually have its own teaching and research hospital, and in 1916, it actively set out to raise money, allocate land on campus, and make plans to build one.

The new hospital, designed by Coolidge and Hodgdon, featured the most modern surgical and medical facilities possible at the time; this complex, connected by long hallways (and/or quadrangles) to scientific and teaching facilities, enabled the university to conduct medical education entirely on its own terms. Coolidge and Hodgdon had little if any experience in hospital design at the time, but they deftly matched the needs of modern medicine to the architecture of the existing campus. Their scheme of long, narrow pavilions was ideal for providing maximum light and ventilation; it could also grow organically and create a series of courtyards and quadrangles.

The nature of the hospital complex—architectural and otherwise—was modified by time, of course. New specialties evolved, and space needs changed in ways that could not be predicted in the 1930s. A layout of narrow corridors was eventually insufficient, for example, to house the almost constant introduction of new medical technologies. And by the post–Word War II period, massive glass buildings with artificial light and ventilation overshadowed the gentle cloistered effect that had been so carefully wrought.

More recent, still newer ideas about hospital architecture have accompanied new developments in medicine itself. A major change in this area is the shift to ambulatory care and the related construction of freestanding buildings. The hospitals—now organizationally separate from the academic university—remain within the interconnected medical center complex, which also includes the medical school. But as medical professionals are experiencing a new period of innovation, significant change can also be expected from the architects who build for them.

42. Albert Merritt Billings Hospital *Coolidge and Hodgdon, 1927*

To establish the medical school that the university's founders imagined, two things were required: a full-time faculty and a hospital dedicated to it. Both requirements came true largely through the efforts of Dr. Frank Billings, whose surname remains on the building that is still central to the hospital complex. Dr. Billings had been dean of Rush Medical School, but when Rush and the university gradually parted ways, Billings sided with Harper's position in favor of a school closely tied to science and research.

When the Rush alliance ended in 1916, Billings became the dean of the university's new medical school. The doctor recruited a full-time faculty and was largely responsible for raising the additional $5 million-plus to build. The main donor for the eponymous hospital was Albert Merritt Billings, the dean's uncle and a founder of Peoples Gas, for whom the hospital is named. As a clear sign of the university's hegemony, Coolidge and Hodgdon, proven masters of the carved-limestone architecture evolving on campus since the years of Henry Ives Cobb, were selected to design Billings.

The hospital's main facade exhibits both the antique stateliness and twentieth-century simplicity that the modern Gothic became known for—an emphatic rhythm of arched windows and prominent buttresses between broad, flat planes. A telling shift in the architecture of the hospital was that it fronts unabashedly on the Midway. While the earlier quadrangles were built around fortress-like courtyards and turned their backs on the outside world, the hospital welcomed it. The courtyard is open on the south, albeit behind an iron fence, and the facade is rigorously symmetrical; these features, quite unmedieval, were signs that the institution was willing and eager to draw the public in.

There was concern at the time among university planners that the hospital's towers should not be too ornate and in no way upstage the dual towers of Harper Library. Billings's "bell towers," as they are called though they actually conceal elevator gear and water tanks, are still prominent and anchor the west end of the Midway, much as Rockefeller Chapel and International House dominate the east. Its undeniably high profile can be interpreted as a desire to be part of the university along with the need for a separate identity.

Beyond its symbolic content, the deep courtyard in front of Billings also signals the layout of the hospital and medical center at large: long, narrow slabs, orthogonally connected, suitable for additions of the same configuration. As the complex evolved, a number of other courtyards were enclosed, some architecturally detailed and some not, but all designed for maximum light and air. Billings naturally suffers from anachronisms, but its architecture still serves as the handsome centerpiece of a great center of healing.

43. Hicks-McElwee Orthopedic Hospital

Coolidge and Hodgdon, 1931

The first additions to Billings maintained the symmetry of the facade and the layout of narrow, orthogonal halls. Hicks-McElwee was carefully harmonized in its massing and style with Billings next door as well as with Bobs Roberts Hospital on the other side of Billings. Beyond its role in research, the building also housed the Home for Destitute Crippled Children (HDCC). The HDCC was a once-independent hospital founded in the 1800s, a suitable affiliate for the medical school since charity work was considered essential to teaching and research. A few years later, private patients were also admitted, though the name remained unchanged. The HDCC later moved around the medical center, following growing pediatric units, and its bathos-soaked name was formally associated with the medical center until the 1980s.

44. Bobs Roberts Memorial Hospital

Coolidge and Hodgdon, 1930

"Bobs," as the building was and still sometimes is called, is a mirror image of Hicks-McElwee but its advent and history are all its own. It was the first children's hospital of the university complex, built with a donation from Col. and Mrs. John Roberts to honor their late son, nicknamed Bobs, who had died some years before of a streptococcal infection. Coolidge and Hodgdon designed the building to harmonize with the rest of the complex, though "Bobs" has some special touches, including a rotunda waiting room in the crux between the two wings.

This rotunda still has some historical features such as bronze reliefs depicting Bobs and his great-uncle, a British officer who was also dubbed "Bobs" and for whom the child was named. Other stately touches in the original waiting room have been either eliminated or diminished such as a

PREVIOUS SPREAD: *Aerial view of University of Chicago hospitals*

Bobs Roberts Memorial Hospital (left) and Hicks–McElwee Orthopedic Hospital (right)

translucent skylight, elaborate floor pavement, and a circular reception desk. Also in the original, large murals on the walls by artist Aldo Lazzarini depicted poems by popular versifier Eugene Field, *Wynken, Blynken and Nod* and *The Fly-Away Horse* among them.

The fate of this space in particular has reflected shifts in taste over the years. By the 1950s, the literary character of the waiting room was changed into a Wild West theme for the young buckaroo. After 1966, when the children's hospital moved to the Wyler pavilion around the corner, the space was cut up into "a warren of offices," as a Bobs veteran lamented some years later.

Old Lying–In Hospital (in front) with Wyler Children's Hospital and Bernard Mitchell Hospital (in background)

45. Old Lying-In Hospital *Schmidt, Garden and Erikson, 1930*

Old Lying-In Hospital, now occupied mostly by administrative units of the medical center, corresponds to the rest of the Gothic-era architecture of the hospital and is mostly indistinguishable from it. An exception is the south facade that runs along the Midway, which is graced with detail not found anywhere else on campus. This includes an open loggia and cloister, which, as a practical matter, increases natural light to spaces within. Light, more than anything, was an obsession of architect Richard Schmidt, who had coauthored *The Modern Hospital*, an authoritative guide to hospital design written in 1914. "Sunlight is now an acknowledged retardant, if not an actual destroyer, of microorganisms," the book states, "and it is highly desirable that sunlight shall enter almost every part of an institution." Also along the south, the second floor opens onto a loggia or shallow balcony, giving the hospital a more domestic than institutional feel. The architects took pleasure in adding small details as well, such as a row of shields over the arcade with the names and dates of legendary women doctors; one is left blank to honor future discovery.

Wyler is notable primarily as an attempt, with mixed success, at finding a modern form that was also harmonious with the Gothic idiom. The building has a flattering profile from some angles; the limestone "fins" that articulate the surface are lively and strong. Schmidt, Garden and Erikson also designed the transitional section connecting the new building with the Lying-In Hospital one door south. Curiously, the section's buttresses and arched windows as well as the building material, Indiana limestone, make it appear a convincing part of the old building rather than the new. This would suggest, among other things, that the virtues of the modern Wyler are at least partly due to the Gothic sensibility of the Schmidt firm, retained in the thirty-six years that passed between its work on Lying-In and Wyler.

Nevertheless, Wyler shows some gross miscalculations of the type that were common in the Brutalist period of the modern era. Critics who regard stone curtain walls as an oxymoron (stone being a weight-bearing, not weight-defying material) will note that these limestone walls do not even create the illusion of load-bearing masonry. And on the side of the building, we see an unintended sign of "function" within: the windows on the first two stories have been replaced with modern thermopane, but those on the top two stories have not. The obvious difference reflects the fact that the first two floors are the domain of the University of Chicago hospitals, whereas the second two belong to the university's Division of Biological Sciences.

47. Bernard Mitchell Hospital *Perkins and Will, 1983*

The most obvious feature of Mitchell is its size. It was part of a $90 million modernization scheme for the sciences and medical center, $5 million of which came from Bernard Mitchell, a Chicagoan who developed industrial equipment such as fluorescent lamps and later founded a fragrance company called Jovan. The hospital named for him more than doubled the bed capacity of the university hospitals to about seven hundred.

This massive colored-glass box bears little relationship to its neighbors, and the building expresses little more than its function as a container of medical technology. Many functions moved to Mitchell from cramped facilities elsewhere. Radiology is concentrated here; Lying-In moved from its old quarters to new ones in Mitchell with the latest technology for infertility treatment and neonatal care. The new Arthur Rubloff Intensive Care Tower, the physical link between Mitchell and Wyler Children's Hospital, was fully outfitted and includes a helicopter landing pad.

Invisible to the naked eye is that this is an early "smart" building with a network of computer terminals, voice-sensitive intercoms, message-transmitting pagers, and computer-controlled pneumatic tubes running throughout. Architecturally, Mitchell is not striking, but its sheer size was much appreciated by many departments of the hospital, which could now spread out and interact with one another with modern efficiency.

48. Duchossois Center for Advanced Medicine

Tsoi Kobis Associates, 1996

The difference between Mitchell Hospital and the Duchossois Center for Advanced Medicine (DCAM) is the difference that evolved in medicine in the thirteen years between the two. The shift was enormous, from an emphasis on in-patient care, which is Mitchell's main purpose, to the growing trend toward ambulatory care, which is served by DCAM. Quite naturally, practical differences between the two have also made them architecturally distinct from one another; the ambulatory care clinic has a prominent drive-up entrance, for example. Other differences between the old and the new could be understood as more symbolic, such as DCAM's glass walls, which are conspicuously more transparent than Mitchell's. In general the trend toward greater patient comfort is unmistakable. "Healthcare design is much more like hospitality design today," says Michael Bush, designer for Tsoi Kobis, architects of DCAM along with Hanson, Lind, Meyer, which did the building's hard engineering.

The exterior gives away no obvious clues that this is a medical facility. A sleek canopy facing the street, a glass tower overhead, polished finishes inside, and ubiquitous natural light throughout make this a welcoming place. An atrium that reaches from the fourth floor to the top is a source of light that also functions as an organizing device. On one side of this grand space are offices where patients meet physicians and undergo examinations. On the other side, treatments and procedures are conducted. Thus, one of the most attractive features of the interior also helps patients know where to go and why.

The hospital's exterior mass was designed to blend in with the university's existing fabric, although the architects were guided by President Hanna Gray's suggestion that the new building recognize the Gothic tradition without simplistically imitating it. The design solution has walls of considerable mass at their base that get lighter, glassier, and more complex with each ascending story, thus following the Gothic formula. The Gothic is just an echo, however, as the repetition of precast concrete panels is a thoroughly modern expression.

Duchossois Center for Advanced Medicine

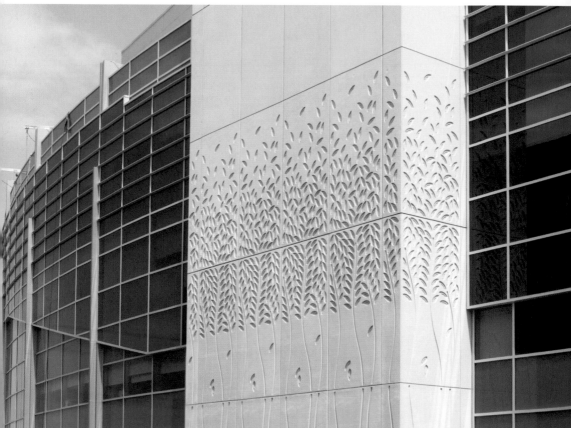

TOP: *Comer Children's Hospital*
BOTTOM: *Comer Children's Hospital, detail of facade*

Comer Hospital, sculpture

It is easy to like Comer, which is brand-new as this is being written, and aggressively cheerful. Its architects, Stanley Beaman & Sears, an Atlanta-based firm, were chosen for their experience in the design of children's hospitals. They understand that children are generally more sensitive than adults to the disruptive effect of a medical visit and also more apt to see through, and rebel against, inept masquerades.

Nature is the overriding motif of this building, which is designed as a "healing environment" for children. Most conspicuous is the leaf pattern imprinted on the precast concrete walls around the base—inspired by the ivy that covers many buildings around campus. Here it "grows" around the building and up the elevator shaft on the side. In the lobby is a large aquarium and a wall fountain with water that cascades over cast bronze leaves from various identifiable trees.

Comer demonstrates that a hospital layout of long corridors and rooms of uniform size may be a thing of the past, celebrating its many functions in the variety of the design. "We are proponents of exploding the core and shifting the walls around," explained Betsy Beaman, who led the design team. The architects have shifted detailed forms, textures, and colors in unexpected ways, too. An example is the main glass stairwell, which is lit with different colors on each floor; from the outside it looks like a rainbow-colored column—a touch that says many things before it says "hospital."

50. American School of Correspondence

Pond and Pond, 1907

This old vestige of the neighborhood is now an official landmark of the City of Chicago, and it appears that the hospital's expansion plans will have to work around it in the next few years. The American School, which was not a part of the university, was an advanced idea at the turn of the century—it offered correspondence courses in subjects as varied as stenography and telephone engineering. The school soon grew to the point that it required this large building, designed by the distinguished "modern" architects who also did the Hull House complex.

Pond and Pond were regarded as avant-garde, although their most aggressive contemporaries, including Frank Lloyd Wright, tended to criticize the antique and conservative look of their work, which ranged from houses to factories. In fact, the Ponds were marvelously original with striking decorative patterns in brick, unique organic ornament, and modern profiles that have no historical antecedents, though they also shared many ideas with Gothic revival architects. Primarily, they were passionate about handcrafts in architecture.

In the American School building, which is now owned by the university and the hospitals, this is apparent in the attention given to subtle expressions in the form and color of brick. A "Gothic" sensibility led also to the buttresses that run up the sides of this building, and the arts and crafts detailing of the lobby inside. The Ponds believed a building was only truly modern if it expressed the hand of the person who created it. To achieve that goal they drew not only from the Gothic, but also from Colonial American brick work and even the polychromatic facades of Venice.

51. Abbott Memorial Hall *Coolidge and Hodgdon, 1927*

Old pictures of the medical center, particularly aerial shots, show Abbott in a more flattering light than it enjoys today. When built, it served as the scientific research laboratories related to the patient care wards at Billings Hospital. Abbott and Billings were the medical school's first buildings, constructed almost simultaneously and illustrating that clinical and research work at this university were indispensable to one another. Initially, the two buildings were not physically connected; they were separated by a fine courtyard with walkways criss-crossing a grassy sward.

A few years later the medical and surgical wings of the hospital were lengthened and intersected with Abbott. And by the 1980s, most of the courtyard space within was built up with more buildings, including the magnetic resonance imaging facility. Today all that is left to see and enjoy is the north facade of Abbott, which was built at the height of Gothic design at the university, with canopied niches (empty to suggest that the building was around for a long time and that vandals have destroyed the sculptures that were once in them) and a pair of university crests, one for the University of Chicago and the other for Rush Medical School, the university's one-time partner in the medical education enterprise.

For years, Abbott's exterior architecture was concealed and relatively forgotten on Fifty-eighth Street, but its charms were given new life in the 1980s when the science quadrangle was newly configured with its main axis terminating at Abbott with a view of its fine arched gate.

52. Surgery-Brain Research Pavilion

Schmidt, Garden and Erikson, 1977

It is quite by chance that this building now finds itself situated at what is in some respects the true center of campus. Opening to a square that it shares with the university bookstore, it is also just across Ellis Avenue from the Administration Building. The pavilion supports a mix of uses, with the lower floors devoted to brain research and the upper floors to surgical procedures that have outgrown other facilities. The building is connected on all six floors to the northeast corner of Billings Hospital, which itself has evolved into a building of vastly mixed uses.

As would be the case with Mitchell, built six years later in the same modernist spirit, there are few exterior clues to the different activities going on inside. Broad "buttresses" that run vertically on the side of the building in reality conceal a heavy-duty ventilation system, de rigeur for biological labs and modern operating rooms. Slit windows are tucked between these broad limestone planes. Perhaps the most articulate element of the Surgery-Brain Research Pavilion is the sculpture outside, a characteristic bronze by the Italian artist Arnaldo Pomodoro. It is an abstract section of a globular object that reveals a complicated, arguably beautiful, interior underneath a more serene exterior.

53. Nathan Goldblatt Memorial Hospital

Schmidt, Garden and Erikson, 1951

This building is indistinguishable in broad outline from most of the rest of the Gothic-style medical center—replete with arches over windows and traceried decoration over the door. Yet it came some twenty years after most of the rest of the limestone medical center. Dedicated to new approaches to the treatment of cancer, the hospital was funded with $2 million from Maurice Goldblatt. The retail magnate had "lost his zest for business," wrote *Time* magazine, after his brother, who was also his business partner, died from cancer. Goldblatt was convinced that cures were on the horizon. Nuclear medicine was in a promising infancy at the time, and when this facility was opened, it was said that the mystery of cancer would be dispelled within a decade. Isotopes, a cyclotron, and radiation treatment were among technologies at the forefront of research into the disease at the time. Curiously, Goldblatt Hospital was also noted for its use of music to soothe patients about to undergo anesthesia.

West Campus

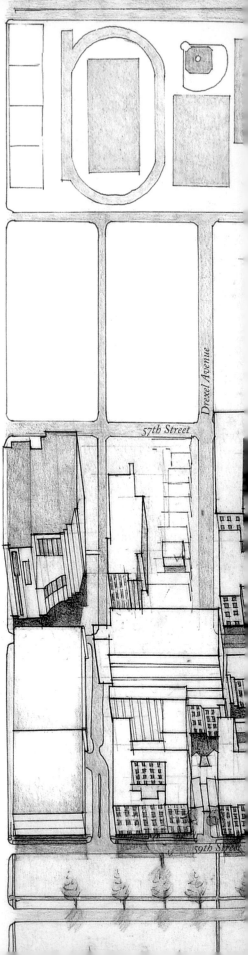

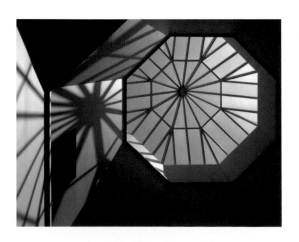

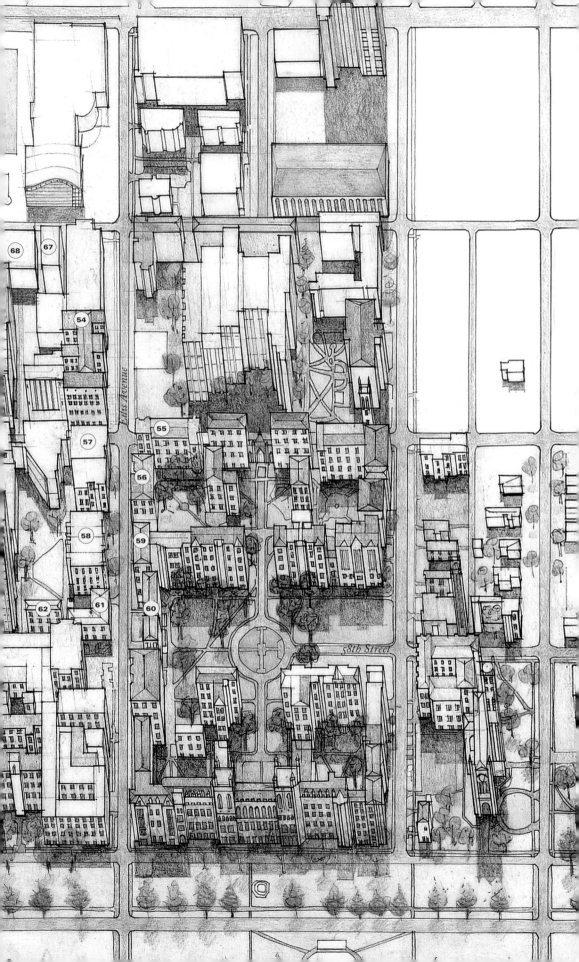

Architecture and Modern Science

When the fledgling university first expanded beyond its original four blocks, it was inevitable, if undeclared, that its science complex would move west and then north of the original quadrangles. This was affirmed when Abbott Hall, built in 1927, went up on Fifty-eighth Street behind the medical center, largely to connect Billings Hospital to the rest of the campus. Still, anything like an integrated complex for science departments was long in coming. It was not before the 1980s that an abandoned steam plant and workshops were razed to make room for the Science Quadrangle, finally realized by the construction of the Crerar Library. Since then other buildings have gone up around the quad and nearby, including the Kersten Physics Teaching Center in 1985 and the Center for Integrative Science (CIS) in 2005.

In contrast to the original quads, the Science Quadrangle was built without too much concern for architectural uniformity. Moreover, at least two of the quad buildings, while arguably inspired in design, came at a time when modern architecture was passing through what can only be called an unfortunate period. The Hinds and Cummings laboratories were designed in the 1960s when the style termed "New Brutalism" was popular. Energetically inconsiderate of neighbors, the Brutalist style consisted of blocky compositions that were largely unrefined and rose up from the ground like a primeval Stonehenge.

This walk will show other examples of the university's attempts to modernize its architecture beyond the Gothic conventions, and it will demonstrate that such shifts in style are essential over time, and that architecture is in many ways an effort to join innovative technologies with up-to-date needs. With the university's ample catalog of so-called modern buildings, we will also see that the range of success and failure in this period was rather wide.

Recently, a new and more sensitive modern spirit has replaced the relative misfortunes of New Brutalism. Context and environment play an ever more important role in twenty-first-century architecture. One of the most recent examples is the CIS, a mammoth structure that is broken down into human-scale parts, including atriums and lounges specifically designed for scientific cross-fertilization. CIS's very size, and its ambition to actually influence the conduct of research, will make its acceptance, or lack thereof, an interesting episode in the story of form and function on this campus.

Research Institutes

The Research Institutes are no architectural masterpieces, nor are they known for their comfort. But these gray limestone boxes have survived for more than a half-century since they were built to house advanced research in biophysics, metallurgy, and nuclear studies. Perhaps the best that can be said about the sprawling complex is that it is nicely proportioned and inconspicuous, but the most interesting thing about the architecture is what might have been.

Before the Accelerator Building, the first institute structure, went up in 1947 (followed by offices and labs in 1950), two members of the physics faculty, George Marmont and Robert Moon, outlined a remarkable set of concepts for their ideal building on the site across Ellis Avenue from Stagg Field. "What will organic architecture do for the scientist?," they asked in a report entitled "Desiderata For a Space to House a Community of Scientists." The physicists described a place with flowing space inside, a light structure of steel frame and glass, and aluminum cladding. They even sketched a streamlined design that resembled Frank Lloyd Wright's futuristic Research Tower for Johnson Wax in Racine.

Such a structure was never built, of course. Instead, departmental discussions of the new building focused entirely on its function, which was initially to house a cyclotron and other accelerator devices that are basic to atomic science. Because exceedingly heavy objects would be moved around inside, the architectural idea was reduced to a "long, rather narrow industrial type building with a heavy crane running the length of the building," to quote a memo of the faculty committee that included Nobel laureate Enrico Fermi. Basic floor plans were also sketched out and handed to the firm of Schmidt, Garden and Erickson, Chicago's leading architects at the time for medical and scientific work. They designed a building that was functional, economical, and entirely (if temporarily) up-to-date.

Limestone was used to harmonize with the rest of campus, though its treatment is flat and lacking in surface ornamentation. When brand-new, the Research Institutes must have looked clean and even sleek, especially when compared to old Stagg Field, a castellated mass then unfashionable and utterly unrestored. Today they represent an architecture of subtraction in search of a legitimate set of modern ideas.

Charles Hitchcock Hall (right) and Snell Hall

55. Charles Hitchcock Hall *Dwight Perkins, 1902*

Hitchcock Hall has nothing to do with science, but it suits this portion of the campus tour as an example of creating something new, architecturally, within the old template. Hitchcock is connected to the conventionally Gothic Snell Hall (designed in 1893 by Henry Ives Cobb), with which it harmonizes nicely though Hitchcock goes far beyond it in terms of modernity. Hitchcock was designed by Dwight Perkins, a distinguished Chicago architect who accomplished the seemingly impossible: a merger of Prairie school with Gothic revival.

The story of this building goes back to the donation by Chicago widow Mrs. Charles Hitchcock, who gave funds to build a men's dormitory to honor her late husband. Initially, it was to be designed by the campus architects at the time, Shepley, Rutan and Coolidge, likely after some Oxbridge model. But Mrs. Hitchcock resisted the choice with a touch of rancor. "I am not content...when I have not been consulted at all," she wrote in a letter to President Harper and instead suggested Dwight Perkins as architect, a compatriot of Frank Lloyd Wright, with whom (among others) Perkins once shared space and opinions in the fabled Steinway Hall studios early in their careers. Like everyone in the Steinway group, Perkins was eager to develop a new style, the so-called "organic architecture," and was an odd choice for the Chicago campus. Before undertaking the project, however, he did travel to Oxford, where he had the opportunity to witness Gothic buildings firsthand so that he might create an organic version.

OPPOSITE: *Charles Hitchcock Hall*

Unlike other dormitories on campus at the time, Hitchcock Hall has several doorways, avoiding the long dreary corridors that accompanied the central-entry approach at the time. Perkins used Bedford stone to conform with the rest of campus, and the horizontal lines of his building, a Prairie trademark, are transmuted into a kind of cloister. His carved ornamental details run up the sides of Hitchcock as extravagantly as in any of its more Gothic neighbors, but the imagery is less European and entirely more Prairie School, with native Midwest plants prominent in the designs. As part of the overall picturesque and asymmetrical scheme of the university, Perkins's building blends in harmoniously and is often praised for demonstrating the versatility of two distinct styles as blended by the hand of a thoughtful and talented architect.

56. Searle Chemistry Laboratory *Smith, Smith, Haines, Lundberg and Waehler, 1968*

In 1968 when Searle was designed and built, there was still no way around the stark modernist rectangles that graced (or afflicted) almost all architecture of the period. Happily enough, Searle's design of anonymous vertical bays makes the exterior as inconspicuous as possible amongst the richer Gothic quadrangles nearby.

This was the first new laboratory building that the chemistry department had occupied in forty years, and the faculty worked closely together with architects Smith, Smith, Haines, Lundberg and Waehler, an old firm that designed early New York skyscrapers in the 1930s before making a name in science buildings. Searle's layout might seem commonplace now, but it was innovative at the time. On each of its four floors, function is served with offices on one side of the hallway and corresponding laboratories on the other. Laboratories are modular in design with temporary walls that can be moved to accommodate larger and more complex instruments. Another strong point of Searle was its faculty offices, which were regarded as more luxurious than in any other building.

An acknowledged defect of the $5.5-million building (with $1 million coming from the family that owned the eponymous pharmaceutical company and most of the rest from the government) is its elevators, which sometimes stop inexplicably at every floor. Occupants say that this problem goes back to 1968 when the building opened and the equipment was misprogrammed because of trade strikes during the Democratic Convention in Chicago. Today, Chemistry is moving parts of the department to the new Center for Integrative Science.

Kersten Physics Teaching Center

57. Kersten Physics Teaching Center *Holabird and Root, 1985*

When Kersten was completed in 1985, there was general rejoicing on campus. The physics department finally had a building that matched its stature and the science quadrangle now had an eastern extremity of architectural interest. Moreover, the building showed that modernism suddenly fit the world that it was being designed for. This is not to say that all other modern buildings on campus are unsuccessful, but most of them, even the respected Regenstein Library, took some getting used to. Kersten, in contrast, got positive reviews from the beginning.

To most of the outside world, the teaching center is inconspicuous, since its Ellis Avenue facade is plain, echoing the proportions and fenestration of Hitchcock Hall across the street. What is most exciting about Kersten is its series of setbacks and terraces which open from large common areas in the building and overlook the science quadrangle. Atop this section is a small observatory with a twelve-inch telescope. Another interesting element is Kersten's three-story spine, a narrow extravagantly glazed volume that bisects the floor plan's two sides and contains an atrium-like exhibition space; its second floor continues over Fifty-seventh Street with a bridge connecting the classroom building to the Research Institutes.

Hellmut Fritzsche, chairman of the physics department when Kersten was built, was very involved in the project, working together with Holabird and Root and the university architect, Harold Hellman, on choosing everything from the modern fixtures for teaching labs, the type and size of blackboards, and the polished wood windows that could be opened to let fresh air in after class.

THE HENRY HINDS LABORATORY
FOR THE GEOPHYSICAL SCIENCES

5734

58. Henry Hinds Laboratory for the Geophysical Sciences *I. W. Colburn, 1967*

There is nothing subtle about the Geophysical Sciences building, yet it suits its functional purpose perfectly. Hinds's exterior is heavy, solid, and earthbound; geologic force could not have been far from architect Colburn's mind as he worked with limestone, brick, and even ceramic building materials. The building is not all brute force, however. Colburn was also in tune with his clients' experiments in spectography, fluid dynamics, and other delicate sub-fields that required specialized and precise laboratory environs.

The architect had to use his powers of persuasion to convince the trustees, who frequently saw the campus in one shade of gray limestone, of his use of brick trim. He argued that the university buildings were not monochrome at all, as the early quads were brightened with red tile roofs— a point that he made with a colorized aerial photo. Colburn's use of red is admittedly less conventional; it looks like an underlayer of brick revealed only where the limestone skin is pealed away.

Finding artistic form to meet all functional needs is a challenge for any architect. Colburn came through nobly, generally speaking, with towers that serve functions—elevators, plumbing stacks, ventilation—but also resemble the skyline of a Tuscan Hill town. To a purist, these might seem out of place on a campus that is marked mostly by the English Perpendicular, but like many of Cobb's and Coolidge's Gothic buildings nearby, Henry Hinds has a medieval tone, however abstract, and reaches undeniably to the sky.

Colburn also won the hearts of the geologists by making room for the Ruth Duckworth ceramic mural in the entryway of the building. This work is an abstract relief map of mountainous terrain, with Mount Fuji as a centerpiece and an array of craters, volcanoes, and other earthlike forms colored with clays, oxides, and other elements.

OPPOSITE: *Henry Hinds Laboratory*

Ruth Duckworth ceramic

59. George Herbert Jones Laboratory

Coolidge and Hodgdon, 1929

It would be hard to imagine a building that blends more seamlessly with its neighbors than this one. In fact, utility rather than architectural statement was what the university had in mind when George Herbert Jones, a founder of Inland Steel, gave money for a new building for the chemistry department, which had been crowded with quarters in Kent Laboratory. One wing of the new laboratory, Gothic in the simplified manner of the 1920s, is connected to Kent. The L-shaped building makes an elegant gesture on the quadrangle with exterior steps and an entrance diagonally astride the crux of the two wings.

Jones is spare in ornament, but variegated limestone blocks give the walls an antique patina. Its arches and lancet windows are restrained but well proportioned, and its simplicity is not stark or conspicuously "modern." The laboratory blends with the elaborately medievalized Kent Hall on one side, while exhibiting affinity with the Administration Building on the other side, built almost twenty years later as a much more extreme case of the modern tendency to strip away any signs of extravagance or the past.

In 1967 Room 405 of Jones was made a National Historic Landmark because it was here that scientists led by Glenn T. Seaborg, later head of the Atomic Energy Commisson, first weighed and examined plutonium, the necessary fuel for nuclear fission. Their discovery took place in 1942 in a six-by-nine-foot laboratory, one of many laboratory spaces in the building,

George Herbert Jones Laboratory

with minimal bearing walls (for expansion) and ample electrical current (which was lacking in other labs). In this and other ways, Jones was a building for its time.

60. Administration Building   *Holabird, Root and Burgee, 1948*

The "Admin Building," as it is called, is hardly the most loved structure on campus. One can only acknowledge that it is a bland lapse in an architectural neighborhood that is otherwise proud and exuberant. One might wonder why the Gothic template was so harshly abandoned when this building—which might have been an architectural centerpiece—was built. There are various reasons, the most curious of which was a lecture by Dr. Joseph Hudnut, dean of the Harvard Graduate School of Design, at the Art Institute shortly after the end of World War II. Hudnut had recently brought the radical modernists Breuer and Gropius to Harvard from Europe and was himself a strong propagandist for a new architecture to express the spirit of the twentieth century. In his lecture he criticized the University of Chicago campus as missing the ancient spirit of Oxbridge while neglecting any mark of a "modern university." This made a big impression on at least one university trustee who had enough influence to pave the way for a stripped-down design by Holabird, Root and Burgee (Burgee was temporarily a partner with the Chicago firm before he joined Phillip Johnson in New York City.) Other reasons for the modern design included the need for economy and swift construction. In addition, the stone-carving trades had become

Administration Building

casualties of time and military service during the war, making too much Gothic embellishment prohibitive. There were postwar steel shortages as well, meaning that the simplest possible construction with outer bearing walls of limestone, bereft of towers and turrets, made modernism a practical solution as well as an ideological one.

The alumni were largely up in arms when the first schemes of the Admin Building were published. One wrote to the *University of Chicago Magazine* that the Gothic quadrangles had "been a source of pride to countless alumni who have had a chance to compare the homogeneity of the buildings with those of other major universities, most of which are an appalling aggregation of everything" architectural. "Let there be a tower," wrote another alum, "a great Gothic tower, tall and slender...taller than the chapel tower, more simply beautiful than Hutchinson."

The magazine went on to publish an "official interpretation" of the design. "The new building will be clean-cut, modern and efficient in its lines, a building radiating hope for the future rather than mere veneration of the past." Distrust of the old style was further promulgated in a subsequent issue of the magazine, in which a distinguished authority on European Gothic architecture roundly thrashed Chicago's version. "No more Gothic, no more Greek, or Roman," counseled this sage. "These times have completed their evolution, our times have other needs, other hopes and rights."

University Bookstore

61. University Bookstore *Shepley, Rutan and Coolidge, 1902*

Originally built for the University Press, this building now houses the bookstore. Built of brick (instead of limestone), its design is reminiscent of old English shop fronts, with two facades divided into three distinct bays. The arcade on street level suggests the covered gallery of a market district. Overhead, gables are simple, though the middle one is more elaborate, resembling something of the (highly mercantile) Dutch Renaissance.

Correspondence about the design of this building suggests that there were thoughts of making it a temporary affair, as classics professor

William Gardner Hale—who built a fine brick home for himself on the edge of campus—warned against this tendency in a letter to President Harper. In any case, the building has enjoyed a history of consistent utility, with the press sharing its space with the Law School until Stuart was completed in 1903; it also made space for the library until Harper was built in 1912. Today, the old place, situated across from the Administration Building, sells books and coffee and has assumed its place as a true epicenter of campus.

62. Ingleside Hall *Charles Atwood, 1896*

Ingleside Hall represents one of the more unusual episodes in the university's history. The building was once the Quadrangle Club and was situated on the corner of Fifty-eighth Street and University Avenue, now occupied by the Oriental Institute. When the institute was being planned and the Quad Club was getting new quarters, Ingleside was moved in 1929. This was not a simple operation. The building was relocated in two parts, and a twelve-foot section from its middle had to be left behind. Its orientation could not be changed, moreover, except at additional risk to the structure, so its original back is now its front facade, which faces Fifty-eighth Street.

The building, originally the work of Charles Atwood, chief designer for Daniel Burnham who also designed the building that became the Museum of Science and Industry and the Reliance Building in the Loop, has lost something in all of these changes, but it is still a handsome structure. Its design is Georgian, simple in mass with a more ornate beaux-arts (now rear) entrance. Ingleside shares the use of brick instead of the dominant limestone on campus with its two next-door neighbors (the Bookstore and Cummings Life Science Center), although this seems to be an accidental coincidence based on Ingleside's past. Today the building serves as the university's human resources department and the campus postal station.

Ingleside Hall, with Abbott Memorial Hall in background

Cummings Life Science Center

63. Cummings Life Science Center *I. W. Colburn, 1973*

Situated two doors west of the Hinds Laboratories, Cummings rises eleven stories, second in height on campus only to the carillon of Rockefeller Chapel. To some, the building represents an unfortunate example of 1960s Brutalism—blocky, unrefined masses that reflected, perhaps not intentionally, the primitive state of modern architecture at the time. From more oblique angles, however, its profile resembles a fortress-like castle on the Italian countryside.

As many professors involved in the planning for Cummings had different ideas for the life sciences building, the ultimate configuration became a cubic mass with laboratories stacked one on top of the other. Among practical considerations was the need for ventilation in experimental laboratories. This also became an artistic opportunity as the forty brick-covered vents echo, however vaguely, the medieval/Renaissance custom of exterior walls that expand out from their base. Functionally, the profile protected medieval castles from intruders; here the stacks collect increasing volumes of stale air as they rise from the lower laboratories to the upper ones.

Similar to his experience with Hinds, Colburn was challenged in his use of brick, usually regarded at this university as suitable for residence halls only. At Cummings, brick provides a sense of age and warmth. To persuade the committee of his choice of building material, the architect prepared two renderings, one with brick, the other with limestone. The one with brick was pictured with a warm blue sky; the one of stone had a sky of slate gray. The trustees predictably chose the former.

64. John Crerar Library *Stubbins Associates, 1984*

John Crerar Library

Despite its massive design, there is something inconspicuous about the Crerar Library. Maybe this is due to the fact that its openings are deeply recessed behind the structure's massive limestone-covered walls. A modernist composition of solids and voids, the library was much appreciated when built for giving shape and an important new purpose to a proper science quad-rangle, which was long awaited in some quarters. The Crerar structure was built to house a substantial science collection of 1.3 million volumes, 700,000 of which came from the historic Crerar library (privately founded in 1897 with the bequest of a book-loving railroad-car magnate). Among testimonies at its dedication in 1984, physicist Albert Crewe said that an obscure book about space-related metals in the collection helped him solve problems in building a high-resolution electron microscope.

Art and architecture critics also commended Crerar when it was opened. Many praised its well-lit reading rooms inside. Others liked the sculpture, *Crystara*, by John David Mooney, suspended in the atrium. Tastes have changed since Mooney's work, a composition of jagged aluminum and Waterford crystal, was completed. Today, the sculpture as well as the building seem a little like gentle refugees from a harsher design epoch. In fact, the Crerar and its fine landscaping outside marked a new beginning on this campus for modern architecture, which in many previous renditions was less attentive to conventional ideas of beauty or comfort.

65. Center for Integrative Science (CIS)

Ellenzweig Associates, 2005

In rare cases academic architecture can express the state of scholarship, and the CIS is one of these examples. In recent years, science has changed from an enterprise largely constrained by traditional disciplines to a process that flourishes best when it crosses these boundaries. Today, key problems are solved at the edges of conventional fields. And this new structure, the largest building ever constructed on campus, was built to facilitate collaboration between the biological and physical sciences. Ellenzweig Associates, the Boston firm that designed this building, was commissioned because of its extensive experience in the design of science and research facilities at Harvard, MIT, and, more locally, the Loyola Medical Center.

Here, the central theme is the integration of common areas where scientists can meet and exchange ideas. Appropriately, the building is bisected by a walkway that serves as a gate into the Science Quad with an axial view toward Abbott Hall's splendid Gothic arch. The CIS also demonstrates that Harry Ellenzweig and his associates have not given up their classic modernist roots. (As a student Ellenzweig studied with Charles Eames and Buckminster Fuller, among others.) There is a certain conventionality to the mostly square boxes and the building's glass-and-limestone curtain walls. But agreeable details show that the architects brought a thoughtful touch to the project. The four-story steel columns, which may seem strikingly large at first glance, effectively break up and humanize the

Center for Integrative Science

TOP: *Green houses on top of the Biological Sciences Learning Center*
BOTTOM: *Donnelley Biological Sciences Learning Center and Knapp Medical Research Building*

otherwise massive block of the building. Some of the walls are entirely of glass, a technique that not only demystifies the goings-on inside, but also enlivens exterior space all around. The building is occupied by the Institute for Biophysical Dynamics, the Howard Hughes Medical Institute, the Ben May Institute for Cancer Research, the James Franck Institute, and the Department of Chemistry, and has enormous underground physics laboratories on two floors with many special features including a vibration-free environment. Atriums, meanwhile, are dramatic, light-filled, and sited where scientists from all disciplines will converge.

Ellenzweig once noted that even though Cambridge had once had second-rate laboratories, the English university produced a long line of Nobel prize winners in science. "They had wonderful tearooms," the architect explained. The University of Chicago now has a building with both unexcelled laboratories and attractive common rooms.

66. Knapp Medical Research Building/Donnelley Biological Sciences Learning Center
Stubbins Associates, 1994

Partly inspired by a desire for a more prominent physical presence on campus, the Division of the Biological Sciences "acquired" this narrow slice of land and raised an enormous multi-use building as a nexus of research and teaching. As it is described in a university publication, the building is "designed to carry the 'one-room schoolhouse' concept into the twenty-first century," combining "a modern medical research center with a state-of-the-art learning center for biology students at every level from undergraduate to post-doctoral."

The Knapp-Donnelley is a building of two parts, one of which is devoted to teaching, the other to research. As this portion of campus develops, the building's long facade will constitute the west side of what is planned to become an extended Science Quadrangle north of Fifty-seventh Street. Knapp-Donnelley is an attractive limestone building and an interesting essay in modernism with an old-campus flair. Gothic ogee arches emphasize its two entrances; the limestone facade features a vertical progression of openings also reminiscent of the Gothic period. Some have the proportions of mullioned windows, and others appear "splayed" and fortress-like. As Gothic architecture generally rose from heavy elements on the ground to lighter ones in upper stories, this building's roofline is charmingly serrated with the gables of glass greenhouses.

High Energy Physics Building

67. High Energy Physics Building *Hausner and Macsai, 1967*

Form and function were blended in a most modern manner in this radically designed building. Its reinforced concrete cantilevers enabled a fourteen-foot-high loading bay and first-floor service entry where equipment associated with quantum physics could be assembled and loaded onto trucks. Among equipment assembled here were spark chamber-counter arrays that were large and heavy and required utter precision and logistical muscle (including a crane) to build and transport.

In the Brutalist tradition, where function is unadorned and raw materials celebrated, High Energy Physics is an interesting exhibit of the fleeting tastes of its day. Outside its design is severe; inside the concrete waffle-slab structural system (for optimal lightness and easy access to utility conduits) is frequently exposed. The architects, Hausner and Macsai, were a relatively unheralded firm despite their mastery of reinforced concrete in this period. They succeeded in moderating the basic brutality of the building with limestone cladding and by tucking it beside the larger and more decorous modernism of the Laboratory for Astrophysics and Space Research.

68. Laboratory for Astrophysics and Space Research (LASR) *Skidmore, Owings and Merrill, 1964*

While the LASR is not a temple of lasting importance, it deserves mention as an essay in engineering-as-architecture. It was designed by Skidmore, Owings and Merrill, who were not only involved in tall commercial buildings at the time (Sears Tower would come a few years later), but also in stretching the limits of long ones. The challenge was increasing the length of structural spans and increasing volumes of space unencumbered by intermediate supports.

Vast unbroken interiors are more important in some kinds of build- ings than others, and perhaps it was not critical here. But who knew what the future would bring? It was impossible to predict how large scientific instruments would become, but the laboratory was designed to accommo- date the future as best as engineering and architecture could do at the time. Besides the classic Miesian proportions of its exterior, LASR's materials of granite pedestal and limestone cladding added to the monumental pres- ence of the building.

Laboratory for Astrophysics and Space Research

North of the Quadrangles

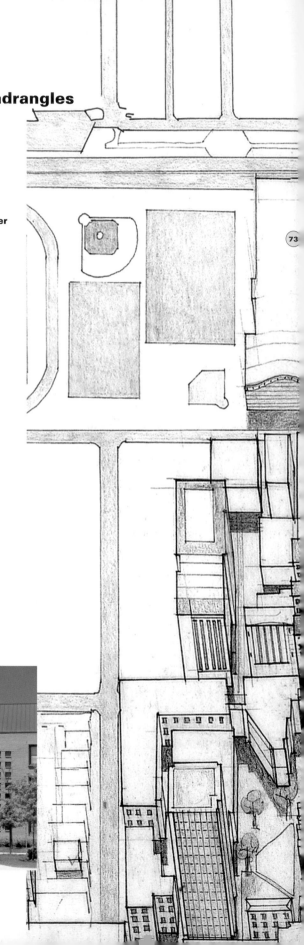

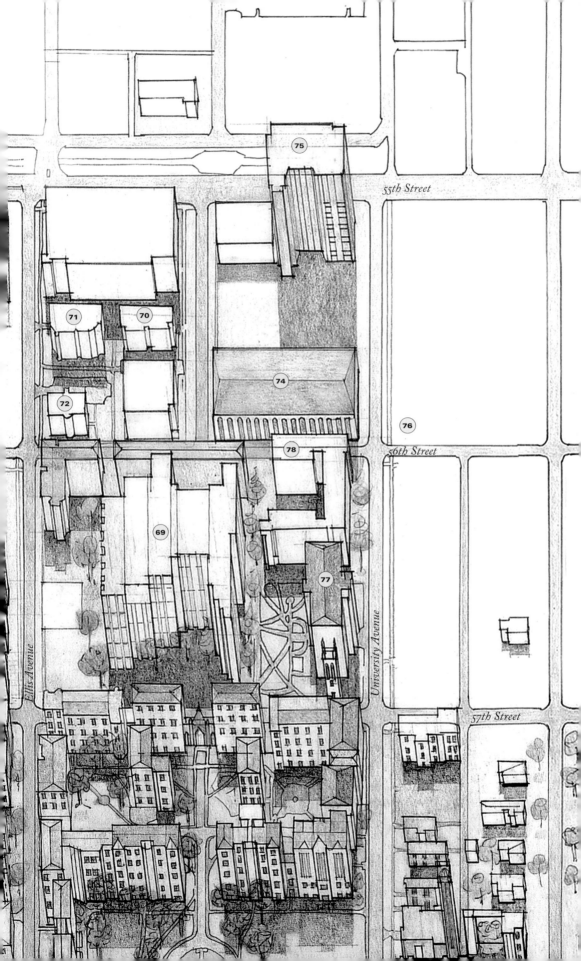

55th Street

75

71   70

72

74

76

78

56th Street

69

77

Ellis Avenue

University Avenue

57th Street

A Village for Students

By the 1960s the university had a bright future to look forward to. It had over-come "urban blight" nearby with the help of various governments and a keen bit of urban renewal. College enrollments, after years of disruption, were ready to double, and the academic departments were enjoying excellent reputations. In addition, in 1965 the Ford Foundation gave $25 million to begin the university's biggest capital campaign to date, called Campaign for Chicago. It came when modern architecture, for better or worse, was in full flower.

With new resources at hand, planners began to imagine expansion in general and development of the north extremities of campus in particular. Among plans for this development was a scheme proposed by Edward Larrabee Barnes, consulting architect to the university at the time, for a "student village" with dormitories and an art complex around a system of quadrangles that would open to Fifty-fifth Street. The Barnes plan, unveiled in 1967, represented an attempt to create a "lively, well-traveled campus," as plans were later described in an article in the *University of Chicago Magazine*. Its openness to the street, in contrast to the enclosed quadrangles of earlier decades, followed a new policy that "privately owned commercial facilities should be regarded as essential ingredients in student life."

While neither money nor enrollment turned out to be sufficient to realize the whole Barnes plan, the 1960s were hardly moribund as far as building was concerned. "Urban renewal," engineered by the university, was in full flower all along Fifty-fifth Street, where old, privately owned buildings were taken down and their land either left or rebuilt with stark modern replacements. Two important modernists at the time, Harry Weese and I. M. Pei, designed scores of private residences in this area, culminating in Pei's design for a mid-rise apartment building nicknamed "Monoxide Manor" for its site on the median strip along its well-motored stretch of Fifty-fifth Street. Weese meanwhile designed Pierce Tower, the university's urban-renewal-style dormitories, while Barnes built the Cochrane-Woods Art Center, an intimately scaled cloister stripped down to bare essentials.

Even though the idea of moving student activity north of the quadrangles proceeded slowly, it was not abandoned. It just took more decades than the early schemers might have thought. In the early 1970s the Regenstein Library went up on the edges of what might have been the student village, and it did succeed in moving the locus of student activity. The Field House, built in 1932, assumed new importance by the 1980s—not because of the Big Ten basketball games that were originally imagined, but because a new fashion for fitness captured students in the years that followed.

Perhaps the area's slowness to develop was in fact a virtue, as it gave a new generation of architects time to develop—to shed the Brutalism of the

1960s and 1970s and to skip the postmodernism of the 1980s and 1990s. In the recent additions to the area north of the quadrangles, Cesar Pelli and Ricardo Legorreta have realized some of the original ideas for a student village. In their schemes, they have overcome the bare-to-the-bone modernism of the previous generation and have also resisted the temptation to imitate the ornate Gothic of a previous, better-loved, age. Instead, a new gym and a new dorm complex have endeavored to do what contemporary design does at its best—to distill the essence of the past and incorporate it into the fabric of the present and future.

69. Joseph Regenstein Library *Skidmore, Owings and Merrill (Walter Netsch), 1970*

The Regenstein Library was conceived in 1965, when the fundraising Campaign for Chicago was being launched and plans were made for an efflorescence of campus construction. To meet a most pressing need, one of the early large bequests—from the family of Joseph Regenstein, a stationery magnate—was slated for library space. The original idea was to build a "graduate library," which would be connected to other libraries (including the Harper Library, which would continue to serve the college) by computers and pneumatic tubes for books.

When the Regenstein was completed, however, usage of Harper dropped off precipitously, as undergraduates as well as graduate students were drawn to the new library. As a result, the campus's center of gravity

Joseph Regenstein Library

was pulled north, due in part to sheer critical mass—the Regenstein was now the largest building on campus. Its design also facilitated the shift, as the deep anterior courtyard was positioned on an axis with Cobb Gate and the Main Quadrangles.

Happily, "the Reg" has gotten consistently good reviews by users, although its aesthetics took some getting used to. Architect Walter Netsch, of Skidmore, Owings and Merrill, at the time was in the throes of an architectural approach that he called "field theory," an effort to apply a certain logic to the seemingly arbitrary shapes that afflicted modern architecture at the time. Briefly explained, field theory created complex geometric forms from simple basic units—small cells assembled into large forms. The theory is not a uniformly successful idea, and it can grow out of control and charmless. Netsch's University of Illinois-Chicago campus was an example of the latter (it has since been renovated and changed), and in his Northwestern University Library, theory sadly overshadows aesthetics. At the Regenstein, however, library director Herman Fussler reined Netsch in specifying something more conventional and "linear." In this more restrained essay, Netsch is effective in creating a large integrated whole out of smaller sections. On most floors, reference collections and seminar rooms constitute the central space, with main stacks and faculty study carrels on either side. All sections are pieced together with conspicuous asymmetry but seeming geometric order.

Field theory is also well-suited to the need for expansion; theoretically, the jagged-edge shape of the Regenstein could take on additions in any direction deemed desirable. Additions are now being planned to extend the library to the west, which may give proof to the field-theory notion that any structure so conceived can grow asymmetrically and organically like a crystal. More down-to-earth, the new addition (to nearly double book capacity to 11 million volumes) will also extend the quadrangle concept with a semi-enclosed courtyard west of the library and Henry Moore's bronze sculpture *Nuclear Energy* (dedicated in 1967 on the site of the first controlled nuclear chain reaction in 1942) as its iconic gateway.

There is nothing particularly Gothic about the Regenstein, though Netsch did apply "an age-old aesthetic attitude that goes back to Gothic Cathedral days," as he wrote. "They took their programs, what the cathedral was to achieve, and used the geometric definition of form . . . as the factor to establish the character and quality of space." While Netsch's architecture can be brutal (in the Corbusian and common sense of the word), the Regenstein Library is commonly regarded as one of his better large buildings, and one is tempted to credit the conservative influence of the Gothic all around (and that of Herman Fussler) for a building that has acquired a measure of beauty that others of the same vintage have not.

OPPOSITE: *Regenstein Library*

Cochrane–Woods Art Center

70. Cochrane-Woods Art Center *Edward Larrabee Barnes, 1974*

In the early 1970s when he designed the Cochrane-Woods Art Center, which includes the Smart Museum, architect Edward Larrabee Barnes was a classic modernist, excited by unadorned beauty and eager to manipulate space in interesting ways. Unlike many of his contemporaries, Barnes discerned that the university's calm Gothic architecture did not clash with these ideas, and in his design for the art-history complex he paid close attention to the existing environment of limestone walls and sylvan courtyards.

The architect is well-known for the IBM building (1983, now known as 590 Madison Avenue) in Manhattan, a soaring bundle of triangles suggesting that the modernist grid is eminently manipulable. In a project close to Chicago, he designed the buildings of the Chicago Botanic Garden; the structure includes a complex of courtyards and walkways to frame and orient the naturalized landscape that surrounds it.

At the university, Barnes's museum and art center seem simple but the design is sophisticated. The gate adjacent to Greenwood Avenue is modest, appropriate to the small sculpture garden inside, which features works of stone and cast metal. A large glass wall to one side reveals the reception area of the Smart Museum, beyond which we can see slices of the art-filled galleries, which are mostly a single space divided by moveable partitions. On the other side of the center are offices and classrooms for art history, whose exterior of smooth limestone panels and punched windows have none of the interest of the museum side—testimony that the design of more utilitarian spaces was a harder problem for modernism to solve than that of flowing galleries.

Court Theater

71. Court Theater *Harry Weese and Associates, 1981*

Harry Weese was a natural choice for this theater, largely based on his work on Pierce Tower nearby, but also because he was experienced in theater design. In 1960 Weese designed the Arena Stage in Washington, credited as one of the first exponents of the "regional theater movement," which was evolving at the time. The Arena required an ultramodern performance space, and Weese proved up to the task with one of the era's earliest theater-in-the-round designs, a stage completely surrounded by audience. At the university the Court Theater is not entirely in the round, but the stage was pushed far out into the parquet with seats arching around three sides. To Weese, this approach was not radical but deeply traditional, echoing the lessons of the Greeks and the theaters they carved into hillsides. Weese's first scheme for the theater was rejected as too big and too expensive. The design was eventually pared down considerably, much to the pleasure of then-artistic director Nicholas Rudall, who wanted something smaller from the beginning. The Court is anything but cramped, however, as Weese was a recognized master of spatial geometry and came up with a successful polygonal configuration, laser-like sightlines, and a space that feels both ample and intimate at the same time.

If there is anything that seems dated in this theater, it is its lime-stone exterior. Like his friend Edward Larrabee Barnes in the arts center next door, Weese used the limestone brushed smooth a la postwar modernism. The result is a first impression of the building that is considerably less charming than the theater that one finds inside.

72. Young Memorial Building *architect unknown, c. 1898*

Constructed originally as a hospital (the Chicago Home for Incurables), the old Victorian building was acquired by the university in the early 1960s. It has served a number of university functions over the years including at one time the Business School foundation. The university Police Department currently occupies the first floor. Young also houses the Office of Facilities, Planning and Management, which means that designs for the gleaming modern campus are shepherded from conception to completion in this building, which is in urgent need of restoration.

73. Gerald Ratner Athletic Center *Cesar Pelli, 2002*

Few contemporary architects are better known than Cesar Pelli, and among the elite, few are more prolific, with his portfolio including Petronas Towers in Kuala Lampur, which outshot Sears Tower as the world's tallest building in 1998, and the residential addition to New York's Museum of Modern Art in 1984. These credentials made the opening of the Ratner Gymnasium in 2002 an architectural event, at least locally. Whether the building stands as an architectural landmark depends, as always, on the test of time.

Pelli is an Argentinean who immigrated to America as a student and absorbed his first impressions of the Midwest while at the University of Illinois. Later he was an apprentice in the studio of Eero Saarinen when the master was at work on the Law School design for the Midway (1959). Pelli shared with Saarinen an "alternate" view of modernism that is based not the Miesian box but designs that combined rational structure with more intuitive ideas. (Examples of Saarinen at the time include the TWA terminal at John F. Kennedy Airport, a poured-concrete building that appears to be taking flight) Like all dedicated modern architects, Pelli is driven by new technologies that lead to innovative form. But unlike many, he approaches each new commission with few enough preconceptions that no two of his designs much resemble one another. The architect is particularly interested in the possibilities of glass, how it opens space, reflects light, transmits radiant color, and otherwise gives an inanimate building a sense of life. Glass is certainly one major object of interest in the Ratner Athletic Center; its great walls of "fritted" glass are treated in a way so that one sees clearly from the inside out in the daytime and from the outside in during the dark.

Almost every major aspect of this building is a function of the lightness and transparency of the material, including its most conspicuous element, the system of pylons and cables that supports the entire structure primarily from above, leaving the long facade open, clear, and free. The

OPPOSITE: *Gerald Ratner Athletic Center*

LEFT: *Gerald Ratner Athletic Center, swimming pool*
RIGHT: *Gerald Ratner Athletic Center, interior*

graceful S-curve of the roof is held up by what is thought to be the first asymmetrically supported splayed cable structure of the United States: the supports in the back bear the main loads, leaving the glass front on Ellis Avenue as unencumbered and crystalline as possible.

While there is plenty of rationalism in this building, down to the exposed anchoring and turnbuckles of the cables, a critic has described Pelli's work as also having a "latent emotionalism," or subtle metaphorical expression. The structure's extraordinarily lean walls, combined with the obvious strength of its supports, can be viewed as an apt symbol for what students and faculty are trying to achieve inside.

Pelli's proclivity for innovative designs that also serve practical function is witnessed in a less dramatic way in the university parking structure across Ellis Avenue from Ratner. One could say that its very inconspicuousness is a virtue, as parking ramps are usually blights wherever they are built. This one is brick with long horizontal openings on each level, and transparent glass stair towers, which are brightly lit at night, a subtle but effective security feature. The ground floor along Fifty-fifth Street is occupied by a restaurant and pool hall, bringing back some life to a stretch that has been lined with chain link since the 1960s. This establishment also features bowling, perhaps a vestige from Hyde Park's past as a mecca for smokey night life. The vintage lanes and old Brunswick pin setters are exposed in a glass wall along the street.

74. Henry Crown Field House *Holabird and Root, 1932;*
Renovation *Holabird and Root, 1980*

Announcement of a new field house was made in 1924, just as Amos Alonzo Stagg's Maroons were winning their last Big Ten gridiron championship. Perhaps the legendary coach and athletic director foresaw

OPPOSITE: *Henry Crown Field House*

the decline of athletics at the University of Chicago, and his plan for a new gym represented an effort to revive past glories. In fact, Stagg and President Max Mason staged a groundbreaking for the building at the corner of Fifty-sixth Street and Greenwood Avenue in the mid-1920s, after which it was decided to postpone construction and increase seating at Stagg Field across the street instead. Bigger crowds for football meant more money in the athletic-revenue fund, from which the planned gym, originally designed as an elaborate Gothic affair, would be paid for.

The football team did not get back on the winning track, however, neither on the field nor at the box office, which is part of the reason why architects Holabird and Root were sent back to the drawing board a number of times to pare down their ideas for a heavily gabled, traceried, and crenellated field house. A second, less extravagant design actually still had many of these elements but Trustee Thomas Donnelley was dismayed and wrote Martin Ryerson, former Board president and still a powerful arbiter of campus architecture, to complain that renderings looked more like a "railway station or an armory" than a proper addition to the university campus. But revenue sports were still in crisis and money still short in 1930 when an even more simplified design was proposed. This one, essentially the building that was constructed, was stripped of ornament save for deeply set Gothic-arch windows.

By this time, reduced budgets had penetrated architecture, and tastes were turning "modern." Well-known Chicago architect George Nimmons praised the Field House design after he saw the latest plans and added, "I believe there is no question but that we have finally arrived at a time when there will be a decided change in the architectural treatment of American buildings...the public has reached a point where it desires change. It seems to have become tired of the old work and to want something new."

The Field House was an expression of function if there ever was one on this campus. Broad and simple on the outside—a shell for ample space inside—the interior is notable mostly for the series of great steel arches that created a freespan space, 160 feet from side to side. The place impressed Jay Berwanger enough to choose to play football at the University of Chicago, where he went on to win the first Heisman Trophy— the true last gasp of football glory on the Midway. But the Field House was also suited to intramurals, which would become more central to university athletics in years to come. There was plenty of room for minor sports even when the portable grandstands were in place for intercollegiate basketball when Chicago was still a Big Ten school.

In the 1970s, a renovation by Holabird and Root made the Field House even more suited to intramurals and softer sports. The gym floor and a running track around it was elevated fourteen feet, leaving space underneath for sports such as squash, fencing, and (in time) the rigors of the treadmill and Nautilis. This work was paid for largely by the Henry Crown family, Chicago industrialists, investors, and former owners of the Empire State Building (which is clad with the same Indiana limestone as is used in this gym and throughout the campus). The Henry Crown Field House remained the university's main sports facility until the new athletic center was built, funded by the Crown family's lawyer, Gerald Ratner, an athlete from the university's Big Ten days.

75. **Pierce Tower** *Harry Weese and Associates, 1960*

Pierce Tower

The most memorable thing about Pierce Tower, the first residence hall built on campus after the Depression, is the story of its funding. Money for the building came from a bequest from Stanley "Schnitz" Pierce, an alum and star Maroon halfback between 1911 and 1913. When he died, he left the bulk of his estate to the university, and while his demands for its use were not stringent, finding the money became literally a treasure hunt. Shortly after Pierce's death, his lawyers found a series of numbers among his papers which they rightly guessed to be the combination to a safe in the shed behind his home. It was opened and inside was a note saying that the money was buried in the backyard. Some vague directions led the hunters to dig under a pear tree where they found $20,000 in gold coins and another note. In time, more than $200,000 in antique gold coins was found buried; this and more conventionally deposited assets brought the Pierce bequest to about a million dollars.

Pierce Tower was clearly a part of the university's urban renewal efforts, which had flattened Fifty-fifth Street—an area that university administrators had identified as a "slum" in need of elimination. All along this central artery of Hyde Park, Harry Weese and Associates designed middle-class apartments and townhouses as well as the new dormitory tower for the university. As part of this development, Pierce's design represents something of a fortress, raised on pilotis or stilts against the urban forces that were thought to lurk north of Fifty-fifth Street.

Weese, who had studied and worked for Eero Saarinen, can be described as a romantic in the guise of a modernist, or perhaps vice versa.

Keck Apartments

While designing Pierce, he would visit the campus, asking about students' preferences and their habits. His aim was to enhance their lives, not make them conform to an arbitrary design. As the story goes, the architect even wanted to know what students wore in order to make sure the closets were sufficient for their needs. Of course, this level of precision was a defect of modernism, too, as haberdashery changes along with other needs and tastes, while buildings stay the same.

  The living quarters were certainly a step up from the basic "slab" high-rise form of the time. On the outside the tower featured bay windows, discarded in modern architecture since the waning days of Louis Sullivan. More daring perhaps was the floor plan with three two-story atrium-style lounges stacked up at the center of the building. Around each were dorm rooms on two levels. In this way Pierce represented a modern manipulation of space that remains unfailingly interesting. The Brutalist structure and stark finishes are less attractive to contemporary tastes.

76. Keck Apartments   *Keck and Keck, 1937*

The Keck Apartments, a private residence on the edge of campus, were the work of a firm that represented one of Chicago's surest modern hands. Keck and Keck was best known for the House of Tomorrow at the 1933 Century of Progress fair in Chicago. In their designs the Kecks always showed that modernism was first and foremost practical. The House of Tomorrow was a polygon of standard-size glass panels, filled with design elements imagined for an efficient future, including a garage for the family airplane underneath.

Solar heat was another design feature that the Keck brothers, Fred and William, increasingly learned to moderate and control. (Their later high-rise apartments on Lake Park near Forty-seventh Street are oriented and fenestrated for optimal utilization of the sun's rays.) A vision of the future was everything to these architects, and in the apartment building of three units that they designed for themselves (and for a professor friend) every efficiency they could devise was designed into the building.

The result is distinctive and "stylistically potent," as a Keck biographer described their work. Inside, built-in furniture kept the rooms open and spacious despite a relatively small footprint. Outside, glass blocks and exterior Venetian blinds made the most of natural light. Everything seems deceptively simple yet masterful, with sheer planes of brick a shade lighter than that of the rest of the neighborhood. But the most remarkable thing about the Keck house are the classic proportions of its facade. They are timeless, making this design appear fresh and advanced even today, nearly seventy years after it was completed.

77. Bartlett Dining Commons *Shepley, Rutan and Coolidge, 1904;*

Restoration *Bruner/Cott, 2002*

In the last few years, Bartlett has been converted from a gymnasium with a running track around the inside perimeter to a dining hall with a varied ethnic menu. Its backyard has been improved greatly; originally the Regenstein's parking lot, it is now a landscaped quadrangle. Despite the recent change Bartlett still harbors truly great memories of old, many of them connected to the days when this building constituted the eastern extremity of Stagg Field.

Bartlett's fine Gothic lines, inspired by Trinity College, Cambridge, in turn inspired the now-demolished Stagg Field grandstands (built in 1914), graced with the same turrets and battlements, which, for old-timers still recall chants that emanated from the crowds ("Chi-ca-go, Chi-ca-go/Chi-ca-go-Go/Go Chi-ca-go ... ") at a time when the Maroons were the scourge of the Big Ten. Intercollegiate football was eliminated in 1939, mostly at the behest of President Robert Maynard Hutchins, who foresaw with remarkable precision the commercial direction of college sports.

But athletics were anything but trivial when Bartlett was built, nor was the athletic director and football coach, Amos Alonzo Stagg, an insignificant force on campus. Thus the building was given importance that is discernible in its finely wrought architecture. The gym was not just a masterpiece of steel framing and limestone ornament, it also received a

substantial interior design thanks to the efforts of Frederick Clay Bartlett, an artist and son of the hardware store magnate, who gave most of the money for the gym. (It was dedicated to the Bartletts' late brother and son Frank, who died while a student at Harvard.)

Bartlett himself painted the murals opposite the front door, done in the conservative pre-Raphaelite manner that was popular at the time. His paintings of medieval athletic contests in fact squared with the Gothic architecture and were highly praised at the time—a local critic compared them hyperbolically to the work of Venetian painter Bellini. It may be that enthusiastic reviews of Bartlett's work had as much to do with his wealth as his tal-

Stained-glass window in Bartlett

ent. But the now-restored murals, dedicated "To the advancement of Physical Education and the Glory of the Manly Sports" and elaborated with raised gesso and gold leaf, are today a pleasurable memory from the past and perhaps an inspiration.

Once notable (but now in storage) was the stained-glass window above the front entrance, depicting a scene from Ivanhoe in which the knight is crowned for his triumph in a legendary twelfth-century tournament—the most substantial work of glass art on campus. Designed by Edward Sperry, a former associate of the studio of Louis Comfort Tiffany, its opalescent and rippled-glass techniques were Tiffany trademarks. Tiffany's own absence as designer is curious; a story goes that he was asked to discuss the commission at a meeting where Bartlett stole his thunder. Thereupon Tiffany simply recommended Sperry and went back to New York.

With so much antique ambiance, it is easy to forget how modern and up-to-date this building was in 1903. Besides its fine arts-and-crafts decoration, its steel ceiling trusses were fully exposed over what was the gym floor and is now a dining room that holds some seven hundred undergraduate diners. Iron staircases, visible through windows from the outside, rise conspicuously through the free space inside.

In recent years, the university honored the heritage of Bartlett in various ways. On the first floor, the meticulously gold-leaf lettering of past record-holders and champions in sports such as badminton and bowling

OPPOSITE: *Bartlett Dining Commons*

LEFT: *Max Palevsky Residential Commons, interior detail*
RIGHT: *Max Palevsky Residential Commons*

have been retained and restored, along with a sign and an arrow directing visitors to the "Football Office" where one of the nation's great college teams was managed. Another throwback, even more ironic, was when in 2004 a team of undergraduates cleared the lounge furniture from the running track circling above the dining room floor and challenged the one-hundred-year-old building record in the mile, which now stands, and will probably remain, at four minutes and thirty-seven seconds.

78. Max Palevsky Residential Commons

Ricardo Legorreta, 2002

It is not surprising that the design of the Legorreta dorms—three separate buildings housing mostly first-year undergraduates—is controversial. With its simple forms and bright pastels, and some seven hundred residents, the big and colorful complex has been compared by students to a prison from the world of Ken and Barbie. When Palevsky opened, the *Tribune*'s critic unfairly blamed its defects on the tendency to hire "starchitects" who will bring flash and fame to campus architecture but not function for the ages.

In fact, the colors of Palevsky Commons—bright purple, yellow, and pink—are not disagreeable, coming mostly from details and interior finishes of glass towers and lounges whose lights radiate strongly at night. Beyond

Max Palevsky Residential Commons

the color issue, the interiors function well with spacious two-story common areas, ample courtyards, and suites that seem to suit the lifestyles of the twenty-first-century college student.

Ricardo Legorreta's name had been advanced for this project by members of the Pritzker family (university benefactors and founders of the preeminent Pritzker Prize for Architecture). He might have seemed an unconventional, even unlikely choice at first; the selection committee of administrators, trustees, and faculty was well aware that the architect's past work was largely in his native Mexico and entirely in warmer climes.But his familiarity with the campus and its neighborhood was undeniable, and his design definitely developed themes already powerful in the existing university context. Courtyards are one feature, and these are carefully drawn to provide privacy and openness for students. (A fine section of the Regenstein rises dramatically over one courtyard wall.) Another is the orange brick that Legorreta used. The architect had been impressed by the richness of brick in the neighborhood, and his brick is just a shade brighter (more tropical?) than the orange-red brick in the Keck residence a few yards away. In addition, the dormitory's windows resemble in form and proportion those of the Research Institutes across Ellis Avenue. These small nods to the neighborhood are not obvious and may not be noticed at first. But they suggest that a building that seems initially strange and out of context may in the fullness of time contribute positively to the architectural fabric of the neighborhood.

The University Neighborhood

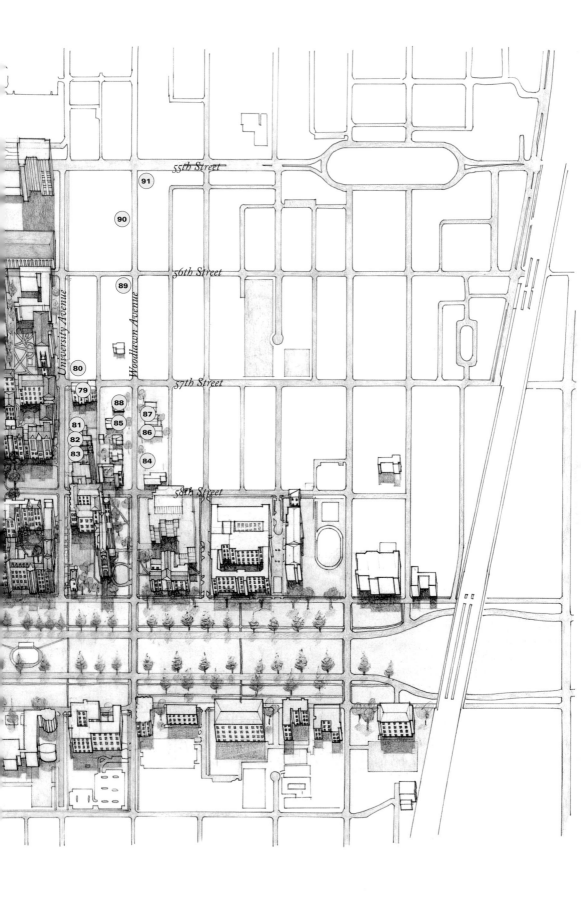

The Progressive Neighborhood

How Hyde Park lives—and lives differently from the rest of the world—remains a subject of continuing fascination to Chicagoans at large (and Hyde Parkers themselves in particular). What makes Hyde Park distinct is, of course, the influence of the university, and that influence is wide-ranging and subjective. Yet architecture is often revealing of character, and at the end of the nineteenth century and the beginning of the twentieth, many houses that lined the streets near campus were a vivid expression of individuals who chose to live there.

Frank Lloyd Wright's Robie House is the most extreme example of a house built for a progressive client. But other houses, particularly on Woodlawn and University avenues, also reflected the free-thinking professors, progressive neighbors, and the architects they chose to build their houses. Many architects working in Hyde Park at the time were associated with what became known as the Prairie School. This term, now familiar but relatively unused until the 1960s, identifies a style, mostly residential, that was considered modern, comfortable, and morally advanced in the period when the university's neighborhood was established.

Wright remains the best-known Prairie architect, though the so-called school was an eclectic group whose similarities are not always obvious. Their history can be traced to the 1890s when a number of young architects, including Wright, Dwight Perkins, the Pond brothers, and Myron Hunt, shared studio space in a Loop office building called Steinway Hall. Many got their early commissions in Hyde Park, of which some seemed more "Prairie"—meaning more like Wright's designs—than others. But in general, all of them designed houses that they regarded as progressive and "democratic." And all would have described their work as "organic," which for them meant architecture that is deeply inspired by its place and the people who lived there.

For many reasons, Hyde Park became a natural arena for these young architects. Today, the neighborhood constitutes a veritable museum of houses with diverse personalities but definite unifying characteristics such as simple form, decorative brick, and frequently the facade of the house turned to the side and not oriented toward the street. This last feature, more a local quirk than doctrine, represents a practical touch in a place where narrow lots made it convenient to defy the older fashion of symmetrical facades.

Modernity rarely went unchallenged, of course. Even Hyde Parkers who considered themselves liberal were "scandalized" when Wright designed Robie House. And in many houses we see a deliberate reversion to old forms and sometimes even a reaction against architecture that seemed overly progressive. It should not go unnoticed that the most successful architect in the neighborhood, Howard Van Doren Shaw, who also had been a denizen of

Steinway Hall, worked mostly in styles inspired by old Europe. Many clients were reassured by such tradition, an insight that led Shaw to choose the role of, as a friend once put it, "the most radical of the conservatives and most conservative of the radicals."

79. Quadrangle Club, 1155 East 57th Street

Howard Van Doren Shaw, 1920

Quadrangle Club

The Quadrangle Club is a place of scholarly distinction, but there is also something cozy and domestic about this private club for university faculty. The design of the building is a masterwork of an architect who was associated with the Prairie School but not entirely of it. Howard Van Doren Shaw had designed many homes for professors and other Hyde Park families when the Quadrangle Club commission came to him, and most of these, while modern in some aspects, were inspired by Gothic or Georgian models.

It was not without some dissension that Shaw was hired to design the club. Thomas Chamberlin, a geology professor and leading faculty member, often rallied against too much attachment to the architectural past and warned the club against its Tudor-style arts-and-crafts design. He even drafted an alternative scheme to present to his fellow members, but at the meeting where Shaw was given the commission, the professor was not even allowed to speak.

In fact, Shaw's style reflects pre-Raphaelist flourish—a longing for the age of chivalry and respect for the old masonry and handcrafts. Predictably, the interior trim is carved limestone, and the floors are of polished flags. But as always, Shaw designed with a light touch. As he wrote in a published description of the club, he wanted "enough English Collegiate feeling to satisfy those who asked for this, and yet enough character of its own, not to suffer by comparison with the ornate stone buildings across the street." The club is of "Harvard brick," as he called it. The gabled roof line is asymmetrical and antique in profile, but the large flowing spaces inside are up-to-date, if not modern, with natural light flooding

in from the stairwell in front and an array of south-facing windows
in back.

In tone, Shaw achieved something serious for an intellectual institution, but with comforts that would suit its members. The dining room has
been the setting for discussions on a high level; legend has it that a lunch
conversation between an archaeologist and a physicist led to the Carbon-14
dating technique. And a classicist once wrote that he was having trouble
understanding Einstein's Theory of Relativity until a lunch companion
"made the whole thing crystal clear, and he did it in a few words while he
was buttering a roll."

Like any club, this one has endured its share of unbecoming conduct, such as the black-balling of a would-be member in the 1930s because
he was a declared pacifist. Women were barely tolerated for years; they
were initially granted only secondary membership and then asked to forego
lunch some years back when the dining room grew too crowded. But time
has been good to the Quadrangle Club and its now-venerable clubhouse.
It has even seen the revival of a rather unscholarly tradition, the *Revels*
variety show on the low stage in the dining room. As in the past this show
is once again well-known for its performances.

80. University Church, 5655 University Avenue

Howard Van Doren Shaw, 1923

There is nothing modern about this building unless it was a modern skill to
understand the past deeply enough to use its parts to create something
new. The University Church consists of medieval elements massed
together, at random but in a picturesque manner, like a medieval enclave. A
narthex-like entrance, tall mullioned clerestories, a parapet overhead, a flattened pediment, and a courtyard open to the street are all woven together
in this relatively small church. Shaw not only miniaturizes these Gothic elements but uses them in ways that have no direct model. Yet the building
appears as ancient and unmannered as if it were many centuries old.

OPPOSITE: *University Church*

81. W. G. Hale House, 5727 University Avenue

Hugh Garden, 1897

This house was built for Professor William Gardner Hale, a professor of Latin who was born in Savannah, educated at Harvard, and taught at Cornell before coming to Chicago in 1892. Even in the 1890s, and even with the large salaries that President Harper paid to attract top scholars, the Hale House was larger than a typical professorial dwelling.

It was designed by Hugh Garden, one of the era's more versatile designers, who was known for his ability to render facades of charm and originality—some modern and some less so. This one followed the traditional tastes of a scholar of classical language and literature. Much of the Hale House is unabashedly Georgian in form—Georgian being in high favor

W. G. Hale House

among many American architects in search of a true national style. With classical care, the architect gave the Hale House an elaborate entrance with a large mullioned window above the front door. But in the spirit of modernism he was exceedingly spare with ornament everywhere else. The exterior walls are plain and articulated by a succession of slightly staggered planes; windows are set in shallow arched recesses. The subtle effects of this design were probably more apparent on its original site facing the street at the other end of the same block. When the Chicago Theological Seminary was built on that corner in the 1920s, the Hale House was moved, turned ninety degrees, and tucked into one of the deep and narrow lots that predominate along the street.

82. Herrick House, 5735 University Avenue

Hugh Garden, 1901

Robert Herrick, novelist and professor of rhetoric, would have been counted among the more pronounced social reformers at the university. He was not shy about stating his views on social greed and injustice, nor on the university's shortcomings, for that matter. Herrick's *Memoirs of an American Citizen* (1905) fictionalizes the rise of a tycoon from humble beginnings to rapacious power. And his novel *Chimes* (1926) is set in a fictional American university of high prestige but dubious merit which in its architecture attempts but fails to emulate the warmth of "the lovely intimate quads" of Cambridge.

The house built for such a person would hardly be expected to express retrograde values, and this one, though ample in size, is indeed as stark as they come, lacking even modest decorative touches such as shutters. The interior holds pleasant surprises, however. Calvert House (a Catholic student organization), which occupies the building today, has maintained the beautiful arts-and-crafts woodwork and painted tiles of the original interior.

Vincent House

83. Vincent House, 5737 University Avenue

Howard Van Doren Shaw, 1897

Professor George Vincent, a sociologist, first met Shaw when both were at Yale, and soon became friendly with the architect. After designing Vincent's house, Shaw went on to become the architect of choice in the burgeoning neighborhood. (He later grew into a similar role as architect to North Shore plutocrats.)

Shaw's architecture was well suited to many Hyde Parkers, who appreciated his lovely exteriors, which straddled the line between convention and experiment. In the Vincent House we see a definite preference for the stately colonial profile that the aggressive "moderns" (such as Wright) actively disparaged. At the same time, the design is stripped down and abstract—as if the elements of a conventional Georgian house had been disassembled and tastefully reconstituted to suit the site. Vincent was not Shaw's first client in Hyde Park, but he was certainly an influential one. He became dean of the faculty and certainly recommended Shaw to others who wanted something in the modern direction but with reassuringly traditional elements.

84. Roche House, 5725 Woodlawn Avenue

Rapp and Rapp, 1900

The Roche House would fit harmoniously in most wealthy neighborhoods of its era, but here it seems almost overcrowded with classical and Georgian ornament. The owner, John A. Roche, was a politician, a former mayor of Chicago; and the architects were among Chicago's leading theater architects. Given this cast, its nonmodern flourishes are predictable enough. The heavy cornice, scroll pediments, and the mix of Ionic and Corinthian orders in the design were traditionally dignified touches and exactly the kinds of elements that modern architects were rejecting at the time. Nevertheless, the Roche building is not without inventive elements: in a neighborhood where many houses were oriented not toward the street but to the side, Rapp and Rapp simply gave the house two facades—one facing the front and the other to the right.

Jordan House

85. Jordan House, 5720 Woodlawn Avenue

Myron Hunt, 1898

What is fascinating about the houses on Woodlawn Avenue is less the radi-
calism of any one design (Wright's Robie House being an exception) than
the way modern ideas became commonplace here at an early date. Designs
that may have been individually remarkable on the drawing board quickly
became harmonious and positively conventional members of the neighborhood. This is also true for the home of Dr. Jordan, an early researcher on
the subject of typhoid whose work led to the project of the Sanitary and
Ship Canal. (The doctor's across-the-street neighbor Arthur Mason went on
to develop the cranes that made the canal possible.)

     The Boston firm of Hartwell and Richardson was involved in the
design, but the main architect was Myron Hunt, a member of the Steinway

group with Wright, Shaw, the Ponds, and others. The house's decorative brick work and shallow recesses make its elegant proportions notably understated. Yet to imagine Hunt's design next to the standard Queen Anne style that was ubiquitous in many other neighborhoods in Chicago, is to get an idea of how radical the Prairie School was in the late 1800s. Hunt later went west to Southern California, where he practiced a craftsman style, the Prairie School's California variant. (He would also become the architect of the Rose Bowl Stadium in Pasadena).

86. Mason House, 5715 Woodlawn Avenue

Howard Van Doren Shaw, 1904

Mason House

This house was built for Arthur Mason, who became wealthy as a result of his invention of crane equipment that was used to unload the holds of ore boats and was important in the construction of the Sanitary and Ship Canal. (The new canal made it possible to reverse the flow of the Chicago River in 1900.) If the inventor in Mr. Mason was progressive and the tycoon in him more traditionally minded, Shaw's design can be seen to reflect both qualities. The house is noted primarily for its reposed facade, which is balanced, stately, and solidified with limestone trim. Yet it has inventive elements, too, such as the use of unadorned planes and unexpected Gothic carving in otherwise classical ornament. Most curiously, the third and top story of the building appears to be a floating mass above the cornice and columns that frame the first two. Devoid of ornament and with prominent eaves overhead, it looks like a dreamy country cottage set atop the Masons' entirely down-to-earth townhouse.

87. Wiles House, 5711 Woodlawn Avenue

Dwight Perkins, 1901

Wiles House

Designed by Dwight Perkins, who also designed the ornate Hitchcock House on the quadrangles, the Wiles' home shocked the neighborhood when it was built. "Plain almost to the verge of baldness," was how Perkins's fellow Prairie architect Robert Spencer described the house. This was largely by way of praise in an article in the magazine *Brickbuilder*, widely read by architects of the arts-and-crafts movement. In fact, Perkins's articulate brick surfaces are the only decoration this house received. Arched recesses around windows and a large projecting bay give it form, and a cornice atop gives it finish. In Perkins's hands the sparest details and careful proportions render this house, built for an attorney and his wife, a handsome container for light-filled interior space.

88. Goodspeed House, 5706 Woodlawn Avenue

Howard Van Doren Shaw, 1906

This house serves as a conservative comparison to other, more modern houses in the neighborhood, some of them also by Shaw. With dormers on the roof line, large shutters on the second floor, and a Palladian window over the front door, Goodspeed House might go scarcely noticed except that it highlights the truly modern elements in some of Shaw's other designs. The conventional Georgian exterior of this residence is memorable for its careful proportions. The design reflects the largely conservative make-up of the client, Professor Edgar Goodspeed, a specialist in Semitic languages and a leading scholar of the New Testament.

Goodspeed House

LEFT: *Hyde Park Union Church*
RIGHT: *Ingalls House*

89. Hyde Park Union Church *James Gamble Rogers, 1906*

Rogers, a nationally famous architect who also designed the first buildings for the Laboratory Schools, must have been pleased to receive what was probably the most important non-university commission in the neighborhood. Rogers was a true eclectic of his era and could design with great facility in a variety of different styles. For the Union Church he came up with a handsome Richardsonian structure. This style of massive stone walls, prominent gables, and thick supporting arches was made popular by Henry Hobson Richardson of Boston; in the late 1800s the so-called "Richardsonian Romanesque" was regarded as a distinctly national style symbolizing strength, immovability, and originality.

A distinctive feature of this church is its large amount of stained glass, filling the sanctuary with abundant light and rich color. Stained-glass windows were created periodically from the time the church was built until the 1960s and represent a variety of ideas about the craft. One curious juxtaposition is on the north wall with a Tiffany-designed window donated in memory of President Harper and another designed by C. J. Connick in memory of Ernest DeWitt Burton, Harper's successor as president of the university. Harper was a spender whereas Burton was a saver. Tiffany and Connick were both distinguished in stained glass but differed greatly from each other, too. While Tiffany "painted with light" and created shades of color and perspective by layering colored glass, Connick's designs (he also designed the window over the chancel in Bond Chapel) were more traditional, using smaller pieces of glass that produced a flatter, mosaic-like effect.

90. Ingalls House, 5540 Woodlawn Avenue *Holabird and Roche, 1906*

With great flourish, the Ingalls House employs the local convention of turn-ing its facade to the side and the side of the house to the street. This siting is made more salubrious by the fact that its double lot actually provides a "front yard" to the left. Most conspicuously, the street elevation is centered by a large brick tower, shaped like a Lutyens-style chimney, which pierces the wall with a window at ground level.

91. Apartment Building, 5515 Woodlawn Avenue *Pond and Pond, 1894*

Apartment Building, 5515 Woodlawn Avenue

The Ponds were early modern architects whose background was in the arts-and-crafts tradition (which also spawned Wright and his compatriots). While they were emphatic about modern ideas such as avoiding excessive ornament, the Ponds were still inspired by tra-ditional forms and handcrafts, which they rendered in unique and abstract ways. The central tower of this six-flat residential building pays homage to the stone carvers and brick masons whose work also inspired British modern architects such as MacIntosh and Lutyens.

Irving and Alan Pond had excellent progressive credentials, including early work in the studios of Steinway Hall with Wright and other Prairie School architects. They were deeply involved in Hull House for which they designed the gabled brick com-plex (largely destroyed except for an older Victorian structure when the University of Illinois-Chicago went up on Halsted Street). In 1904 Irving wrote a seminal article in *Architectural Record* that introduced the design of the Austrian and German Secession movements to America. When the brothers designed this apartment building, it was one of the first structures on this section of Woodlawn Avenue, and the plain flat surfaces and substantial asymmetry of the building were considered quite avant-garde at the time.

Tending to reinterpret older and more traditional forms, the Ponds were criticized by self-professed radicals such as Wright and Louis Sullivan for being too tied to history. But the brothers remained true to their ideas. Beneath the ivy that covers these walls today one notices the architects' love of patterned brickwork, inspired by the English arts-and–crafts, and the classical scallop shell above the door. But the floor plan, which is simple and designed for maximum air and light, is pure modernity and shows why the Ponds, somewhat forgotten today, were highly influential in their time.

Buildings Off Campus

There are several university buildings that are not on the Hyde Park campus but deserve note as architecturally and historically important structures. Gleacher Center (1994) is one of the most prominent, if not tallest, new buildings in Chicago's Cityfront Center on the Chicago River east of Michigan Avenue. The Gleacher Center, which was designed by the Chicago firm of Lohan and Associates, houses classrooms of the university's Graduate School of Business and Graham School of General Studies. The design of Dirk Lohan, Mies van der Rohe's grandson, is a deliberate blend of masonry inspired by the Hyde Park campus and the glass-and-steel modernism associated with Mies. Its Gothic-like elements include east-facing windows with the proportions, if not the craftsmanship or flourish, of decorated windows on many campus buildings. Its glassy volumes are partially cantilevered and some appear to float in midair over the edge of the river.

In Williams Bay, Wisconsin, the Yerkes Observatory was dedicated in 1897 after astronomer George Ellery Hale convinced Chicago "traction king" Charles Yerkes to buy the university a forty-inch refracting telescope, still the largest such instrument in the world, and to build an observatory to house it. University Architect Henry Ives Cobb was chosen for the commission, and since this building was not on campus but on Lake Geneva where the air was clearer for nocturnal observation, he created an arching Romanesque design with two domes, one of them ninety feet in diameter. The observatory's terra-cotta ornament is highly detailed and includes countless creatures (real and imaginary), signs of the Zodiac, phases of the Moon, and other embellishments on cornices, columns, arches, and capitals. Although it is no longer used for astronomy and the land around it may be sold, Yerkes will certainly survive as a museum or as something else that makes use of its scientific heritage and historical importance.

In Luxor, Egypt, Chicago House remains the Oriental Institute's distinguished center of Egyptological research in the shadow of some of the richest archaeological sites on earth. Founded in 1924 by James Henry Breasted, who also founded the Oriental Institute, Chicago House has been the research home of many great Egyptologists. The original house and library complex were built mainly of wood and mudbrick. In 1931 it was replaced with the present facility of stone, baked brick, and reinforced concrete. Its architects, L. Le Grande Hunter and L. C. Woolman, were modernists. The building's traditional arches, arcades, and garden-filled courtyards are alloyed with the modern massing of interlocking cubes and large wrap-around steel windows.

Selected Bibliography

Scores of books and hundreds of articles have been written about the university and its buildings. Among the most useful for a general and curious reader:

Calvert Audrain, William B. Cannon, and Harold T. Wolff. "A Review of Planning at the University of Chicago, 1891–1978." *University of Chicago Record*, April 28, 1978. A concise review of planning at the university as it grew from a few sparsely built quadrangles to a major example of American campus planning.

Jean Block, with photos by Samuel W. Block Jr. *Hyde Park Houses.* Chicago: Universtiy of Chicago Press, 1978. Indispensable as a resource of neighborhood architecture and history.

Jean Block. *The Uses of Gothic.* Chicago: University of Chicago Press, 1983. This is a concise and illustrated history of the campus from 1891 until the 1930s, after which "Chicago Gothic" gave way to modernism.

D. J. R. Bruckner and Irene Macauley, editors, with photographs by Patrice Grimbert, Jose Lopez, and Luis Medina. *Dreams in Stone.* Chicago: University of Chicago Press, 1976. Primarily a picture book illustrating the exquisite virtuosity of the architects and craftsmen who built the oldest sections of the campus.

Thomas Wakefield Goodspeed. *A History of the University of Chicago: The First Quarter-Century.* Chicago: University of Chicago Press, 1916. This detailed history of the university's early years was written by a key trustee, secretary of the board, and member of the buildings and grounds committee. Goodspeed spends much time on the development of the quadrangles and its buildings.

Donald Hoffmann. *Frank Lloyd Wright's Robie House: The Illustrated Story of an Architectural Masterpiece.* New York: Dover, 1984. This is an excellent portrait of the classic Prairie school house.

Julius Lewis. "Henry Ives Cobb and the Chicago School." A.M. thesis, University of Chicago, 1954. This is the only existing monograph on Cobb and includes interesting details about his University of Chicago days.

William H. McNeill. *Hutchins' University.* Chicago: University of Chicago Press, 1991. Among many books and memoirs by faculty, this one captures lively elements of the campus and its environs between 1929 and 1950.

Eero Saarinen. "Campus Planning: The Unique World of the University," *Architectural Record* (November 1960). This is Saarinen's most concise description of his view of the university campus and his plans for it as consulting architect.

University of Chicago. *One in Spirit: A Retropsective View of the University of Chicago on the Occasion of its Centennal.* Published by the University of Chicago Library and the University Publications Office, 1991. This book is rich in photos and narrative about the university's growth over 100 years.

University of Chicago. *A Walking Guide to the Campus: The University of Chicago.* Published as part of centennial celebration, 1991. A brief and useful guide to buildings on campus with architects, dates, and a few details.

University of Chicago Library. *Life of the Spirit, Life of the Mind: Rockefeller Chapel at 75.* Published to accompany a Special Collections exhibition about the chapel, 2004.

The Gleacher Center in downtown Chicago